Tales of
Mr Explorer

Mike Helliwell

Grosvenor House
Publishing Limited

This book is published by
Grosvenor House Publishing Ltd
Link House
140 The Broadway, Tolworth, Surrey, KT6 7HT.
www.grosvenorhousepublishing.co.uk

A CIP record for this book
is available from the British Library

ISBN 978-1-80381-750-7

Contents

1

Introduction

I decided to write the "Tales of Mr Explorer" after having a full knee replacement which restricted my travels. It gave me an opportunity to provide a written account of my adventures for my children and grandchildren to enjoy in the future, encouraging them to explore the wider world.

Hopefully these tales relate some of the interesting moments I experienced during my adventures including instances of awe, enlightenment, fear, my stupidity, human kindness, deep sadness as well as huge joy.

Why Mr Explorer?

My daughter is a primary school teacher and I often go into school to support her teaching. I talk to children, aged between 4 and 6, about animals and the world. My character name is Mr Explorer.

The children get very excited when Mr Explorer comes to school.

I started this as a 'bit of fun' for both me and the children. However, talking to the teachers they told me they get a lot of positive opportunities from these sessions. Children, especially the disruptive ones, become engaged with the subject and the teachers use this as a teaching tool for weeks afterwards. I now see this as more than just fun but 'giving something back'.

In one lesson a year 5 boy put his hand up at the end of the lesson and said, "When I grow up, I am going to be Mr Explorer".

Severe Dyslexia

I was diagnosed with severe dyslexia when I was at university. My university friends would frequently 'rib' me about my many spoken

English mistakes as well as grammatical written errors. These were all in good fun, without malice and I took it 'on the chin' in good humour however, occasionally I did find it tiresome.

Once I was diagnosed it had a massive effect on my confidence and self-esteem as prior to that I always felt 'stupid' especially at school but now I had a reason why I made these mistakes.

It is inevitable this book will have some grammatical errors but what matters, in my mind, is it 'contents and meaning'. I think that is true of the world it doesn't matter if you have a disability, different ethnic background or have little material wealth – it is the 'contents' of the person that matters.

How did I manage these trips?

All my adventures are accessible to many people in the UK. Most of the trips were booked through specialist wildlife companies offering opportunities to potentially see amazing wildlife in remote places. They would source remote accommodation, appropriate vehicles, often 4x4, and expert local guides. This made accessing wilderness areas 'doable' in a c2 week holiday from work and at an agreeable price. Yes, these are not cheap but more practical than trying to do it yourself in a short timescale.

I love wilderness and wildlife, and this is the most practical way to see it and using local wildlife guides massively increases your chances of success. You also have the bonus of meeting local people living a more traditional lifestyle in remote villages.

I did have a reasonably paid job, but I prioritised my spare money for my trips. I don't buy expensive clothes or any clothes, much to my wife, Sarah's, horror. I don't buy electronic gadgets (my mobile is from the dinosaur age) or drive expensive cars. My bonus from work went towards my trips which was my priority for personal expenditure. I was also lucky to have generous holiday entitlement which allowed me to have family holidays and every 2 years or so, my lovely wife allowed me to go travelling anything from between 1 and 3 weeks with the occasional longer trip up to 3 months.

Sarah, my wife, is also very understanding of my hobby and very accommodating with my desire to travel. I thank her and dedicate this book to her.

2

How did my desire to travel, experience wilderness and viewing wild animals get started?

On my mothers' side we had distant relatives in Australia and every Christmas my Grandparents received a letter from ...... THE AUSTRALIANS. It was like the Royal Family writing to us.

The family would spend days talking about it and when I was younger would show me on the map where Australia was. This, coupled with my natural interest in geography I was hooked. So, I had a dream to go, but every young child has a dream, so what made me do it?

Whilst at University as part of the course I completed two, 6 months, placements in industry to give us a 'taste' of business. My reaction to working in business was – it can wait – yes, I will need to get a 'proper job' sometime, buy a house etc, but it can wait as I've got 30 years to do that. So, on my last placement before the final year – I decided I am going travelling for a year – I also asked Sarah, my future wife, to come with me to carry the bags!

Obvious location – Australia.

However, going on a gap year in 1982/83 was 'no mean feat' and 'unheard off', as no-one did it as it was so expensive and was not a 'thing to do' as it is now. The airline ticket in 1983, for 1, was £747.

You can now fly there cheaper more than 40 years later.

Sarah decided to come and for 12 months we worked hard, saved hard, never going out and lived on the 'bread line'. Then we went.

My favourite place which had a 'long lasting impact' on me was Kakadu National Park in Northern Territories, a vast wild and pristine wilderness. We booked a 4x4 safari travelling deep into the wilderness, wild camping by small lakes, swimming underneath large waterfalls and spotting wildlife including many saltwater crocodiles, dingoes and huge number of birds including very tall cranes and storks.

We also travelled through the desert, wild camping beneath the stars, to visit Ayers rock including climbing it, as in those days it was still accessible. I fell in love with the Australian outback and its wildlife. It gave me the desire to continue to travel and explore various habitats around the world.

3

Bravest thing I have ever done

Background

Sarah and I were on our gap year and decided to circumnavigate Australia using the Greyhound bus that followed the coastal road. I say, 'road', from c400 miles north of Perth to Townville in Queensland it was, at best, a rough dirt track. Thousands of miles of open bush country without human influence except the occasional petrol/food stations. Stretching over this c3,000mile track were c10 small villages and Darwin city at the very North. The bus went twice a week – you could get off at any point and the catch the next bus 3 or 4 days later (bus trips, between villages, ranged from 8 to 36 hours, with more frequent stops at petrol/food stations).

We had decided to stop at Derby a small community deep in the outback with no obvious attractions apart from Geikie Gorge National Park (Kimberley) where we could see Johnstone freshwater crocodiles, birds and stunning scenery. The National Park Rangers offered a boat trip once a day on the river. Unfortunately, Geikie Gorge was 170 miles from Derby, so we needed to hire a car.

Prior to Derby we camped on a tropical beach near Broome which is only 300 miles from Derby. At the campsite we met two young ladies who were also interested in seeing the gorge and would be happy to share the cost of car hire. Luckily, I managed to contact the Pub in Derby, which was also the campsite owner, and secured a car hire.

The Greyhound bus dropped the 4 of us outside the pub at 10pm, in the middle of the bush, and we set up camp, in the dark, behind the pub. We soon realised that the Pub was everything in Derby as there were only c6 other houses spread out over a large area and that was it. We had a couple of days relaxing, bush walking and clearing millions of ants from our tent much to Sarah's delight!

We had the car for 24 hours and needed to drop it off, the next evening, outside the pub (on the far side of the road) at c9pm to catch the next Greyhound bus due in at 10pm. We had a great day at Geikie Gorge and surrounding areas.

Dropping the car keys off

One of the young ladies and myself went to drop off the car keys whilst the others finished packing. As instructed, I parked the car on the far side of the road from the Pub, however, this was no ordinary road. It was c50 metres wide and was built to allow the huge 'Road Trains' to deliver cattle to the nearest port 3 miles away. Not really a port, just two huge concrete blocks and a ramp, no buildings, fence or people.

We started to walk towards the Pub and outside sitting peacefully were c30 Aboriginal men and women drinking Sweet Sherry straight from 1-gallon bottles. They hooked their thumb in the handle at the top and then raising their elbow poured the liquid into their mouths, drinking sherry like we drink beer.

As we approached two of them jumped up and the lady gave the bloke a 'right fist' straight into his jaw (I would have been very proud of that punch). Immediately all the others jumped up and start fighting .... oh s***.

The young lady with me said "lets run back to the car" and I replied "NO, we would never make it". I knew we could not run, why I don't know, but just knew if we ran, they would turn on us like a pack of wild animals.

The only option I could think of was to 'bluff it out'. So, I grabbed her arm and pulled her along.

"Just look as though you own the place, keep your head up high, keep looking forward and DO NOT make eye contact.... just keep going".

At this point we were five metres away and they stopped fighting and parted so that we could walk directly to the pub. The young lady was shaking but I was unbelievably calm. We had to walk through a tunnel of c30 people, all agitated and pumped up, spread out over 10 metres glaring at us. As we entered the centre of the group I expected 'a rain of blows' to descend, "keep going and stand tall" I commanded.

Nothing happened, we were through. The Pub door was opened by the landlord with a large glass of whisky.

He said "**That is the bravest thing I have ever seen**"

"We had NO CHOICE if we had turned, they would have hunted us down like rabbits"

"Agreed but bloody brave and the whisky is on the house". Unfortunately, I didn't drink any of the whisky as my nerves kicked in and my arm shook so much, I spilt the full glass of whisky onto the floor.

"No worries I will get you another and this time I will put it on the bar". As soon as we had entered the Pub the Aboriginals started kicking hell out of each other – men and women and by the looks of things equally matched.

"So, what happens now" I enquired with a shaky voice.

"The riot police are coming, there is a regional station 10 miles away, this occurs every couple of months. I have let the Greyhound driver know he has 4 passengers to pick up, but he will not wait for you if you are not there (due to the trouble), you meet him at a lamp post 600 metres down a track at the back of the Pub. You will have to walk down the track in the dark, but the moon is out so there should be enough light – and there is only one lamp post so you will not miss it. AND you need to go now"

So, I drank my whisky, met the others and walked through the bush and after ten minutes we came across the 'one lamp post' by the side of the coastal track. In the background we could hear multiple police sirens.

And within minutes headlights appeared and we were away.

4

Discovering a small herd of Elephants not seen for over 2 years

Background

My first specialist wildlife trip was to Tanzania when I was 30. Sarah was happy for me to go, by myself, as she understood my desire to see Africa despite her being 6 months pregnant.

It was a mixed group of 10 who were all very keen naturalists and on day 1 we set off to a small National Park called Arusha. This was like an introductory safari with few large animals such as Giraffe and Buffalo supported by many different birds and a few monkeys. It was famous, in the past, for having a large Elephant population but due to heavy poaching there has not been any reports of Elephants for over 2 years.

Wildlife guides/drivers

We had two 4x4 vehicles with two very different guides;

One young keen and enthusiastic and the other older and more experience.

We had been in the park all day and were beginning to head back to the Hotel, a 2hour drive away, when I spotted, in the distance, a small herd of Elephants. I called out to the driver to report my findings.

Unfortunately, the Elephants were among trees and below the skyline c3 miles away and no one else could identify them including either of the drivers. After a few minutes the Elephants moved into a large gulley.

My driver, the older one, was very sceptical especially given the heavy poaching, however, the other driver was keen to investigate and wanted to drive around for a closer look. They both got out of the vehicles and walked a short distance away and had a blazing row, eventually the younger driver persuaded him to give it ago.

After driving for c10 minutes we came to the general area where I had seen the animals. Of course, no Elephants. 20 minutes or so we searched – still no Elephants.

As I was the only one to see them people started to doubt me, and muttering began – my credibility was sinking fast. Lucky after another few minutes' wait and personal anxiety, 4 Elephants emerged from the trees and started feeding 200 metres away – I was relieved.

The older driver turned to me and said:

"Good eyes" and a nod of approval...... a proud moment.

The drivers reported to the sighting to the Park Authority who were very interested. They had seen some evidence of their tracks in the last few days, but it was the first confirmed sighting that Elephants had returned to the park.

5

Making friends with a Manta Ray

I was on a whale watching trip from Bali to Komodo Island with the opportunity to watch Komodo dragons. Just south of Komodo Island is Manta Alley, which is a known place, in diving circles, for a reliable gathering of Manta Rays. However, as it is a remote area it is rarely visited so we had the place to ourselves.

The Manta Rays hang around a huge rock that juts out of the sea. There is a very strong current running next to the rock but behind the rock, outside the current, there is deep water, c50 metres deep with heavy swell but little current. If you stay behind the rock, you are relatively safe but if you get caught in the strong current, you would be swept out to sea within minutes – so it's quite dangerous.

The Manta Rays swim with the strong current and then move into the quiet water where 'cleaner fish' gather to eat parasites off the Manta's. It is a 'cleaning station', one of relatively few known cleaning stations in the world. The Manta Rays attracted to this station are the Ocean Manta, which are the largest species with the biggest known ray measuring nine metres across its wings.

We swam in the Manta Alley twice, the first time the swell was very strong and threatened to smash us against the cliff, so most of the poor or medium swimmers decided it was too much for them. A couple of us stayed and I identified 8 Manta Rays swimming back and forth allowing the cleaning fish to clean them up, the rays were 10 to 15 metres down. Visibility was very good, so you had a reasonable view.

Due to popular demand, we decided to have another go the next day as the swell had dropped. The swim was like the day before, swimming up and down alongside the cliff edge watching Manta Rays swimming below us.

BUT I had a feeling that something was behind me – I turn around and three metres away, at the same level, was a huge Manta Ray swimming towards me. Can you imagine not looking and stepping into the road to find a huge bus is coming at you from three metres away – this is what it felt like. A huge beast with a huge open mouth swimming straight at me, the mouth was two metres wide and 0.6 metres high.

The ray moved slightly to one side when it reached me and then slowed down holding itself in the water watching me, we then swam together very slowly up and down. For at least 40 metres I swam next to his eye, one metre away, looking at me whilst I was looking at him. I could have got closer but had to keep moving away to ensure I didn't touch his wing. I try not to touch wild animals in case it spooks them. I turned around as I was approaching the fast current and swam back along the rock face, the Manta turned and continued to swim next to me.

At one point the ray was swimming so slowly with me that I managed to dive underneath it and swim forward so that I could take an underwater photograph of the ray with the surface of the water above me. This was a brilliant experience, so close and for at least 15 minutes, he was clearly wanting to see what I was doing. I was isolated from the others by c100 metres and after a while some of them realised I had a friend and managed to have a quick look before he dived.

It was a very personal experience, for some reason he befriended me and stuck close to my side. Manta Alley is a rock in the sea just south of Komodo Island in a wide bay which is open to the Ocean swells – a bit wild but beautiful.

Manta Rays, in the open Ocean, will often jump out of the water sometimes flipping over and landing with a huge splash. I have also seen them jump or fly out of the water and do a full 360' turn in mid-air before hitting the water. It is amazing to see them fly. Why do they do it? No one knows.

Komodo Dragons

One of the key reasons for the trip was to see the Komodo Dragons. Thomas, my son, had seen them so I had to go, I couldn't be out done by my son!

Komodo Dragons mainly live on 2 Islands in Indonesia the main one called Komodo the other is Rinca, there is also a small population on Flores. Because they are famous, people want to see them, however, due to the remoteness of the Island they only get few visitors – the visitor centres, on both islands, were excellent – on Komodo Island there would be 40 visitors in total and on Rinca just us.

Komodo had a several villages and at the visitor office, basically a mud hut, and they had a small covered market, which was very well done. The sellers had to stay in the covered market, so not hassling you, but also ALL the T shirts and crafts were locally made. Nice people who enjoyed chatting with us. The guides were good and allowed me to take my time whilst making sure we or the Dragons don't get too close to each other. All they had was a large stick with a fork at the end to trap the Dragon's head, for our party of 10 we had 3 guards. What was excellent was they didn't mind if I took my time taking photographs even when the others had walked off.

The dragon is the largest living Lizard in the world – up to four metres long and weighting up to 20 stone with a massive body, big head and long thick tail – the thickness of the body is unbelievable. The world population is c7,000, which is now expanding as it previously dropped to under 2,000 in the 1960's. The population has always been restricted even though they have no natural predators – it is the Apex creature.

The Komodo Dragon's main prey are Deer, Water Buffalo and horses (which have been introduced and gone feral). Dragons actively hunt their prey by hitting them with their tail and then biting them. The Dragons are famous for their toxic saliva, if bitten the victim usually dies of blood poisoning within hours.

However, all these dragons looked harmless and dopy, most just sleeping or watching us especially those next to the homes. However, something did not add up.

Next day we sailed to the south end of the island away from the normal tourist place to small bay called 'Horseshoe Bay' where we stayed the night (on the boat). We boarded a small rubber boat and set sail for the shore but stayed on the boat four metres from the beach. At the top of the beach were seven Dragons and once they saw us, they came running to the shoreline – all excited and curious.

These dragons moved at pace and were very wake and alert – different animals altogether. You would NOT land on the beach with these dragons.

So, I asked the leader "Obviously, those near the visitor centres are being fed daily to keep them dopey". He grinned "Yes, of course, it would be too dangerous otherwise, that why I have brought you here to see the 'real' ones".

We had two trips to see the dragons on the beach – it was excellent watching them watching us and licking their lips (they smell with their tongues, so they were sampling the air to identify the smell) as they saw us as potential prey.

We sailed to within four metres of the beach and the boat man got into the water to hold the boat – in a metre of water. The dragons loved it, especially when we threw a small pebble onto the beach, and they came racing into the sea and one of them swam towards us. I have never seen a man move so fast as he jumped on board, shouting "Quick keep your hands and feet within the boat" as his colleague started the engine to pull away but not before the dragon was within a metre of us – excellent.

I joked to the team "you can imagine being shipwrecked and after a difficult and hard swim avoiding sharks you land on Komodo Island, thinking you are safe, to be met by the dragons" yet c10 miles either way you would be safe as those islands don't have them.

Village on Komodo Island

I felt sorry for the children from one village that was situated next to a large Mango swamp. You can imagine the lecture the mother gives when the kids are going out to play.

"If you are playing football watch out for the dragons and if you are going swimming watch out for the seawater crocodiles in the mango swamp but don't too far out because of the sharks and if you are coming back after dark watch out for the snakes"

"Yes mother" they would sigh having heard it many times before.

6

Witchcraft, in rural Africa, is still practised and more importantly believed

Background

On the second section of my overland African trip between Victoria Falls and Uganda we had a new crew. The guy in charge was 'GP', a white Zambian who was born and raised on a remote farm and had also been a wildlife guide for many years. We got on brilliantly and talked for hours. Sam was the driver who was black Kenyan. He was quiet and kept his distance, his job was to drive and that is what he did.

On the first stage I would often sit in the cab at the front to watch the world go by and talk to the driver about Africa etc. I asked GP if I could do the same. At first, he was reluctant "Sam doesn't like being bothered or distracted from driving" he explained. I said I would be quiet and only want to get a better look at the road.

"Ok I will ask but I'm not promising"

I am in.

My objective was to get Sam to talk about Africa from his perspective but first I needed a plan.

How my plan worked is as follows;

Day 1. Sat in silence for over hour until I spotted what I wanted.

"There a Bateleur Eagle" I pointed to the right, his side of the vehicle.

Sam looked at me "You know what that is?"

"Yes, it is a Bateleur which is small eagle that flies low to the ground"

"Wow" he replied.

We continued, in silence, for the next hour and then I got in the back of the truck.

Day 2. First 90 minutes in silence and then I asked, "Which premiership football team do you support".

"Man Utd" he replied. "Same here, I often go to games. I have not got a season ticket as the waiting list is 10 years, but I have contacts who sometimes pass their tickets on. I go 3 to 4 times a year."

"Wow" he replied, and we talked football for a few minutes and then continued the journey in silence.

Day 3. Silence for the first hour and then he started to ask me questions "Where you from? What do you do? Interested in wildlife?"

But I never asked any questions back

Day 4 & 5. We chatted majority of the time, covering football, his life in Africa, current affairs from both point of views, AIDS, and of course, back to football.

His confidence was gained so I could ask any questions I wanted.

Witchcraft

Day 6.

We were travelling through a heavily wooded area with large mature trees in open woodland – typical seasonal tropical rainforest habitat. By the side of the road, every 20 miles or so, would be bags of charcoal, 10 to 30 sacks, and at one point I saw a car stop and load

2 sacks. BUT there were no people, no houses or villages to be seen for the last c50 miles.

I asked, "Is that Charcoal being sold and where are the people?"

"Yes, it is charcoal, it is the main product around here and the nearest village is about 5 miles that way" pointing to his left deep into the forest.

Being a banker and of suspicious mind I asked,

"Why doesn't someone just load up the car and drive off without paying? No one would know who has taken it"

"It is cursed"

"What! Witchcraft?" I replied astonished.

He looked at me if I was stupid "If you take the bag without paying you would be cursed"

"But how can you curse someone if you don't know who they are or have not seen them?"

Look he gave me was 'are you really that simple'.

"The charcoal bags are cursed, by the witch man every day and anyone taking a bag will carry the curse and that will be transferred to all the people who contact it".

"Wow, do you believe in witchcraft?" I asked.

"O yes, I dare not I have seen people who have been cursed, it is very bad they suffer much pain. You would be stupid NOT to believe" he said in a serious tone.

After a few minutes of reflection, I asked; "So, would be right in saying every village has a chief and a witch doctor and they control what goes on and keep law and order"

"Absolutely, the witch man, we called him witch man only white man call him witch doctor, is often the most powerful person in the village and in villages it helps keep people together" and "You often get women witch men"

Again, moment of reflection. "So, what happens in the city? It is completely lawless in some places with frequent riots and robberies" I had just heard of a recent big riot.

"When people go to the city the process is broken down as they are not controlled by the chief or the witch man, so they do what they like especially if they don't get a job, so no money, no village support.... you are on your own"

7

How I kissed a 45-ton female Gray Whale on the lips – she kissed better than the wife!

Background

I was recommended to go on a whale watching trip to Sea of Cortez in Mexico.

We sailed from San Diego, on a 30-metre sport fishing boat that held 24 passengers, to the Sea of Cortez but first we had to sail 1,000 miles down the Baja California peninsula through the Pacific Ocean. Two thirds of the way down the peninsula we visited a breeding lagoon of the Gray Whale. This lagoon was massive – 10 by 20 miles – with huge areas of shallow water. But first we had to get in, the entrance is very narrow and with the swell it is quite a dangerous operation.

The swell and the meeting of ocean and shallow water provided feeding grounds for large shoals of small fish and of course, huge numbers of birds – terns and gulls and the Magnificent Frigate birds. They look like prehistoric creatures floating some 3 metres above us whilst others were over 100 metres up in the sky – a magnificent sight!

This lagoon is only available for visitors for 4 weeks at the end of the breeding season when all the males have left. Male Gray Whales can be aggressive during this period so too risky for boats. Also, access is limited, by the Government, to one boat at a time with a maximum of 4 in the season. We were there for 4 nights, 3 full days. To explore the lagoon, we were transferred to small boats operated by Mexican fishermen.

What is the lagoon famous for? Close encounters with Gray Whales especially babies who can be curious coming right up to the small boats to have a look at us. Some very curious baby whales even allowed us to touch them, and one let me put my arm into its mouth and scratch his tongue and rub his baleen plates.

But this doesn't always happen and quite often we had to encourage them to come to the boat – they loved being splashed at – my best trick was to get my whole arm in the water and pull it up and down making a huge splash, hard work but very effective as they loved it.

We went out on the Mexican boat for 2 hours at a time and usually every trip we had a baby whale to play with, for c15 minutes, so it was hard work but great fun. Whilst the baby whales came to play the adult female would swim up and down ignoring us. However, quite often a mother would keep their baby away from us getting their body between the boat and the baby.

The very best bit

We were on the water – playing with this baby – rubbing his skin etc – when I noticed the adult female whale looking at me – making eye contact from about 20 metres out.

I will always remember the big black eye looking at me and deciding she may be interested in coming closer, I splashed out to her. She was lying on the surface horizontal to the boat and when I splashed her, she quickly turned to face me and swam slowly up to us and stopped just by the boat.

l leaned forward, stretching out my arms and hands to embracing her and gave her a kiss on the lips.

I have kissed a 45ton female adult Gray Whale on the lips – in the wild.

After the kiss she slowly reversed away from the boat and slowly swam away.

It all happened very quickly, all very smoothly so that only 2 people on the boat saw it the other 2 missed it completely. The Mexican boatman was 'gob smacked'. He told me, in 20 years, had never seen anything like it.

Interestingly if she had mis-calculated the distance and overshot by 2 feet she would have sunk the boat and us!!!

8

The ultimate animal – Tiger

Background

To see a Tiger in the wild is, in my opinion, the ultimate. It is a large powerful creature whilst also being sleek and graceful. The colours and markings are superb. The fact that they live in wooded areas, often in dense cover and because they are elusive, living in large territories, tracking them is a 'real' challenge. Finding Tigers must be my favourite wildlife experience, the thrill and anticipation of the 'hunt', the skill need to find one and the prize is so magnificent.

First Tiger

I have seen 19 different Tigers but the first one will always be special.

My first Tiger was in Ranthambore Tiger Reserve, and we had 'drawn a blank' on the first full day. On the dawn trip next day, we found a young male Tiger hidden in dense undergrowth 20 metres from the track. We watched him for 20 minutes resting on the ground whilst observing the world around him. At one point he looked straight at me, and the sunlight caught his eye, bright yellow, dazzling, it reminded me of the poem, 'Tiger, Tiger burning bright'.

How do you find a Tiger?

They are difficult to find because they are very rare, less than 4,000 worldwide, well camouflaged and have huge territories.

Obvious first step is to go to well-known Tiger reserves where Tigers are regularly seen. There are some reserves in India with large populations, but the Tigers are very elusive whilst in other reserves Tigers have got used to people and this offers better opportunities to see them. Visiting in the dry season massively increases your chances as the undergrowth has died down so visibility is greatly improved and as Tigers need to drink every day, they keep close to waterholes.

Tigers are very territorial, and they constantly patrol the boundary, spraying scent marks, at certain key points, to let other Tigers who wander past that this territory is taken. As a result, you always have a chance as they are moving around albeit most of this activity is at night. Getting to know their habits also helps as they often move around certain areas at selective times of the day. However, territories are huge especially those of the male which can take 3 to 5 days to walk around covering an average of 30 miles a day. It's extremely difficult to find them whilst they are patrolling in the dense woodland.

Luckily Tigers will always take the easiest option when walking around and will often use dry riverbeds, ridges and vehicles tracks where there is less vegetation. Whilst on the move they will often leave fresh footprints reading these can give an idea how fresh they are? Did they pass in the last few hours? Which direction are they are travelling? By following tracks, you can get yourself in roughly the right area.

The crucial bit is to listen to the forest. Can you hear alarm calls from their prey? This gives you an indication that it is around and allows you to focus on a potential area albeit this could still be a relatively large.

Different animals give different calls, and some are more reliable than others. Monkeys and Peacocks are 'nervous and excitable' creatures often giving false calls. Spotted Deer tend to be more reliable as they only call and stamp their hoof when they have clearly seen the Tiger and they have move to a safe distance whilst watching it. The idea being 'if you can see your enemy, it is far less likely to get you, the Tiger you worry about is the one you can't see'.

Then you look, look, and keep looking and hopefully your luck will be in. Having good wildlife guides and drivers help this process but

I enjoy trying to find them myself and trying to spot the Tiger before the guide does.

And when you find one you feel a huge amount of pleasure – well I do.

It is also important to give yourself time. Some tour companies travelling around India will only offer 1 day Tiger watching (dawn and evening trip into the reserve) and fail 90% of the time as they don't allow sufficient time. I would suggest a minimum of 4 days.

If you are lucky you may come across a Tiger that is so confident that it will walk close to the vehicle. I had one Tiger that was so close I could have leant out and stroked it, of course, that would be foolhardy. As the Tiger approached, we all kept very still and silent so not to spook it, as if we did it could have 'lashed out' in panic.

How do Tigers communicate?

Mainly by spraying and scent marking – and then sniffing another Tiger's spray.

Tiger territories are huge and can overlap between females and males but also between females. Adolescent Tigers, without territories, will also wander around trying to find an unoccupied area to potentially set up a territory. Tigers identify set points to spray the urine on, such as a tree stump or raised mound. When they pass this point, they will sniff it to see if anyone else has been around and then spray again.

How do Tigers read the spray?

Basically, Tigers will sniff the scent including pheromones into their nose and then into the 'Jacobson organ" which sits above the nose. Transferring the scent into the organ the tiger face grimaces and this is called the "Flehmen response'.

What does the scent tell you?

- Sex of the Tiger.
- Whether it is ready to breed and, if not now, will it be soon? (females).
- How old it is and what condition it is in. If in peak condition other Tigers will be wary, if in poor condition, it may provide an opportunity to take over the territory.
- Each scent is unique to an individual, so communicating to other Tigers. For example, young Tigers that have left their mothers often come back into the territory so signalling 'who they are' and are not a threat.

By spraying and reading the signals it avoids unnecessary conflict between animals whilst communicating when they are ready to breed.

9

Day I thought I was going to die

Background

During my 'around the world' three months adventure I stayed in the Galapagos Islands for 2 weeks sleeping on a large sailing yacht which carried 16 passengers. Every day was wonderful, wildlife watching, snorkelling and sea trips between stops.

The Galapagos Islands are 600 miles west of Ecuador in the Pacific Ocean. They are all active or dormant volcanos which raise c6,500 metres from the sea floor, sometimes the sea can be 2,000 metres deep within a mile of the island and 6,000 within 5 miles. The Galapagos Islands act as a barrier to the sea currents resulting in rich nutrients coming to the surface, so leading to huge numbers of fish and sea creatures such as Turtles, Sea Lions, Whales etc. In addition, commercial fishing is restricted so the populations are very healthy.

On one snorkelling trip

Overnight the boat had anchored in a lovely bay with 5 miles of sand and on the left-hand side was a huge cliff jutting 1 mile straight out to sea, it was the edge of an old volcanic crater. The cliff protected the beach from the prevailing winds and the ocean, so the sea was calm and beautiful.

The snorkelling party was split into two, strong and less confident swimmers. I was in the strong swimmer party and was dropped off at the end of the cliff and allowed to slowly swim back to shore. Naturally you split up and swim at your own pace whilst monitoring your location and watching where the Zodiac is, in case you need help. Zodiacs concentrated on the less confident party being 600 metres away but maintain an awareness of all swimmers.

The edge of the cliff was the most productive area for wildlife with dense coral and because the water depth was c200 metres deep at the further point there were an exciting mix of ocean-going fish and as a well as reef fish. I swam with many large fish such as large shoals of Barracuda (1 to 2 metres long), Squid, several Turtles and Sharks (Black and White reef sharks, 2 metres long).

It was a great swim and took me over hour to make my way alongside the cliff. As the water shallowed, about 400 metres from the beach, I decided to swim out over the sand to look for String Rays and flatfish which I found several. The water was exceptionally clear, and the sun was over my right shoulder chasing my shadow on the sand and I gradually swam toward the beach in one metre of water.

Suddenly it went very dark over my head, and I could see my shadow became HUGE and long.

Instantly my mind worked out that it was a large shark that had followed me in and now that I was in the shallows, it had decided to attack.

My mind worked overtime – very logical – very calm. I said to myself **"This is it. I am 54 and I have had a good life"** in a relaxed manner accepting my fate.

Then I decided – I not going down without fight, although I knew it would be hopeless, so I raised both thumbs and turned to face my attacker (the idea being to try and get at least one thumb into an eye).

At that point a large Sea Lion swam over my shoulder and put his face 60mm from my mask and snapped his jaws several times and then calmly swam off, I assume laughing to himself. This behaviour is not uncommon having experienced it several times before, however, this time I had not seen any Sea Lions in the bay.

Immediately my nerves kicked in and my 'heart started to race'.

I shouted at the Sea Lion "come here you bugger" whilst waving my arms around trying to punch it.

"You bugger" I kept shouting out.

I staggered to the shore and stumbled up the sand.

"Are you OK? you look white" one of the passengers from our boat enquired.

I told them the tale and basically, I went into shock.

They sat me down, I was 'white as a sheet' and started to tremble all over. After 10 minutes or so my colour and strength came back, and we travelled back to the boat for lunch.

10

Being treated like a VIP

Bharatpur Bird reserve

I was on a wildlife trip in India to watch One Horn Indian Rhino, Indian Elephant and Tigers. At the end of the trip, I went to Bharatpur bird reserve by myself, it is a famous reserve and I always wanted to go.

Bharatpur is a large man-made water reserve, previously it was dry flat semi desert scrubland. However, the 'old Maharajah' was introduced to 'duck hunting' by the British, 300 years ago, and loved it so much he developed his own 'duck pond'. This being India the reserve was dug out by hand and includes lakes, canals and reservoirs to feed the lakes in the dry season. To keep the local villagers and their cattle out he enclosed the whole reserve with a two metre wall. In Indian terms the reserve is relatively small but when you consider it was dug and shaped by hand, it is huge. The reserve is the size of a large town and even supports a Tiger.

I love the place and most of the time I wandered around by myself. I met a local naturalist who offered to show me a large Harrier roost in part of the reserve not open to the public, illegal but why not?

Next day he turned up in a huge old-fashioned car, it looked like an old Humber, and he sat in the front with the driver whilst I had a large backseat. It turned out the journey was 20 miles but took 1½ hours as we drove, for most of the trip, on rough farm tracks and through isolated villages. On arrival we left the car, climbed the wall and then walked 2 miles to the Harrier roost. There was not a lot of wildlife around, but the habitat looked in good condition. The roost was impressive with over 50 birds including Marsh, Hen, Montague and Pied Harriers.

We walked back in the gloom and arrived back at the car in the dark, with only the headlights to guide us. Inside was another gentleman, my guide explained he was a friend, and would I mind if we gave him a lift, why not? The gentleman, who could speak English, explained that the locals had got very excited when they saw the big car and thought I must be an important official. The 3 Indians sat in the front and again, I had a big back seat to myself.

The ride back was brilliant.

Obviously the 'jungle drums' had been busy as when we drove through each village hundreds of children and adults lined the track waving and grinning, waiting for me to pass.

I felt like Royalty, of course, I had to wave back, using the Queens' wave, looking very regal and important, the 3 Indians in the front thought it was great fun.

My hotel was an old Maharajah's Palace, which was beautiful and had a lovely courtyard where you had your evening meal. That night I was the only guest and had 5 servants waiting on me in the prime position of the courtyard, with no other tables.

It just finished off a perfect day.

Blonde Hair

Sarah and I had our honeymoon in India, and we visited a Tiger reserve.

We had several Tigers drives in the reserve but no Tigers. On the late afternoon visit we stopped for a short break close to a small Hindu shrine. The driver informed us that twice a year, for a few days, local villagers visit to leave offerings for the gods, and we were in this period. The shrine was c400 metres away behind some trees and even though it looked insignificant, to us, Sarah and I wandered over to have a look.

Behind the shrine we found 30 or so local ladies about 40 metres away.

We paused. They just stared at us and there was lots of muttering. After a while one of the ladies started to approach us, quickly followed by the rest. We smiled and bowed. They kept staring at Sarah, not me. Eventually one of the ladies touched Sarah blonde hair. They were fascinated by her white hair and many ladies were gently touching it. A few minutes later two men came around the corner, clapped their hands and the ladies quickly disappeared.

11

My best overseas purchase including an 'arm guard'

Background

In 1986 we got married and honeymooned in India. India is my favourite country I love the culture, countryside and wildlife. Best of all I love the people I think they are all barking mad (in a good way).

Which other group of people would:

- Allow Cows to wander into the fruit and veg market and help themselves from the stalls?
- Allow Cows to take priority on the roads even the main ones. All drivers just slow down and calmly drive around, no beeping of horns. If the cow is laying down asleep this could go on for hours?
- Provide cow night shelters with food, in towns and cities, whilst the untouchable people (lowest Hindu caste) sleep rough?

The last part of our trip was a stay on a houseboat for 4 nights, in Kashmir, on Dal Lake. In the evening with no wind and the setting sun it was extremely beautiful.

We hired a car and driver for a full day out into the Himalayan Mountains. After an hour we stopped in a remote village which was holding a religious festival for the month (this is held every 4 years). The village was the starting place for a 6 day (round trip) to an Ice Cave at 6,500 metres which has a huge icicle in the shape of an important Hindu god. (Icicle in the shape of a god – mental).

In the village were hundreds of Sadhu holy men preparing for the trek. We loved Sadhus with their colourful clothes and face paints and ultra-cool attitude.

Whilst we were watching the Sadhus there was a commotion on the road behind us and everyone (all Indian as we were the only foreigners) parted to allow 5 dusty men to march through. They were all walking bare foot, at a decent pace and covered in dust and dirt. Further investigation, by our driver, revealed that they had set off, on foot, from South India 2 years ago and had walked the full way relying of the generosity of the local people.

As I said 'Mad as Hatters'!!!

We then drove to a small stable in the mountains and had a horse ride, for 2 hours, in a large pine forest. It was a still day so very quiet and peaceful. It was then a three-hour drive home through thick pine forests when we came across a small clearing with c20 small workshops all making **cricket bats.**

"STOP" I yelled, we must go and have a look.

Each workshop made a cricket bat, in full, from the local pine wood. They cut, shaped, pressed and made a full bat, they were delighted to show me around. These bats were sold throughout India and pine is the traditional wood used in India rather than willow in the UK.

Of course, I had to buy one. So, I chose the most expensive which cost less than £2.

I was delighted.

We flew back home from Delhi after spending an additional night in the capital. The flight home was early, so it was a very early taxi ride to the airport. I oversaw the heavy bags and Sarah in-charge of the cricket bat. We checked in and upon handing over the luggage Sarah declared "I have left the cricket bat in the taxi."

"WHAT"

Having calmed down I decided to check in first and then go and find my treasured cricket bat. On leaving the terminal I asked a friendly

Indian, where do the Taxis go after dropping people off. He told me that Taxi drivers generally meet downstairs underneath the terminal which you can access via a stairway, approximately 200 metres away.

"However, Sir it is not suitable for foreigners" he pleaded with me as I set off "It will be right" I replied with a shrug of the shoulders.

Walking down the stairs I was met with a sight I couldn't believe. It was huge and dark with thousands of Taxis and people all milling around with several bonfires to keep people warm or to make Tea.

After a lengthy pause to take in the scene – I decided I had 'nothing to lose', so I carried on. As I arrived at the base, I was immediately surrounded by c50 Indian men – "Can anyone speak English" I shout above the dim of 50 men all talking at the same time.

"Yes, Sir" cried one as he pushed himself to the front. I explained the situation, bowed many times to the crowd, which now numbered over a hundred who all bowed back.

As I climbed the stairs, on leaving, I thought – 'No chance of seeing my bat again'.

Back at the terminal we went through to the departure lounge after going through security and passport controls and sat in a huge lounge. 30minutes later the public address system announced, "Could the person looking for a cricket bat please show himself".

I stood up and at that point;

The Taxi driver came through the door, 50 metres away, with my cricket bat held out in his arms and flanked by two tall soldiers in full parade uniform and each carrying a submachine gun on their chest.

They marched across the lounge and the taxi driver knelt and presented me with my beloved cricket bat. I bowed and said thank you. I had some Indian money left over, so I gave him the lot. It was around £20 – the guy nearly fainted.

After composing himself he bowed and said, "thank you", and as he walked backward to the door he kept bowing and repeating, thank you, thank you, thank you.

How much was £20 worth to him? – maybe 1 month's salary, maybe more, not sure. BUT I was happy, and he was happy (assuming the soldiers didn't take it from him!)

The punchline to the story is:

In those days I used to play for a local cricket team and carried my new bat to the middle with pride.

First ball was wide and pitched up – I took a big stride down the pitch 'middled the ball' and instead of shooting off for a boundary it rolled 30 metres.

Bat was rubbish – but it still has pride of place in my bedroom – 35 years later.

Another great acquisition on my travels

Dolly

Equally exciting was the discovery of Dolly who has pride of place in a custom-built display cabinet in my home.

When I was whale watching in Mexico in the famous Gray Whale breeding lagoons, we had a walk on the beach. I was wandering around the dunes when I found a complete Bottlenose Dolphin skull. I showed two friends, I had made on the trip, and they suggested I take it home.

So, I did.

But this is a World Heritage site, so it is illegal to do this. To keep it secret from the crew, guides and the rest of the passengers we gave it a name 'Dolly' so we could talk about it in code.

After leaving Mexico I planned to stay for 4 nights in San Francisco before flying home. I packed her securely in my case before smuggling her home. However, I did have some fun going through the internal airport between Los Angeles and San Francisco as I was expertly guided away from the queue for a 'one to one' with a plain clothed security man who politely asked me "Could you please step inside this room, sir".

Before I knew what was happening, I had gone from the main flight queue to an isolation room being searched. I noticed as the officer was searching inside my rucksack, he was more interested at looking directly at me and making small talk about my trip. I decided the best approach was to do the same. I engaged in conversation and made full eye contact for long periods.

After c10 minutes he relaxed and said, "Nothing here, you are clean have a good trip". Because we were getting on so well and he was particularly interested in my whale watching experience, I asked why I was bought in here.

"The lady at the 'check in' thought you were particularly rough and dodgy"

"So, how many do you search in a day" I enquired.

"Oh, no more than 3 a week, about 1 in every 50,000".

"So, I did look dodgy" saying with pride.

"Oh, yes sir you were pick out as a prime drug suspect".

Interestingly, was it because I had spent 2 weeks at sea getting up at dawn and being on deck all day OR anxious about smuggling in 'Dolly' or a combination of both? I think I was not too worried about Dolly as it would have been, at most, a fine and a slap on the wrist, but who knows?

Dolly got back safely and has its own bespoke display cabinet.

Dolly is also in my 'Will'.

Jessica, my daughter, will inherit her when I die. Thomas, my son, will get the family shotgun.

Both will share ALL my wildlife photographs. However, there is a clause written in the Will. If they dispose of them, lose them or destroy them they MUST give ALL the money they inherit to charity. The Lawyer writing up my 'Will' had to keep a straight face as both Sarah and I played it very seriously.

12

Violent Grandmother from Wigan – in a mini skirt

On my overland trip through Africa the last stage was a short trip through Uganda to watch the Gorillas.

Due to the famous TV clip of David Attenborough sitting with the Gorillas lots of people, who generally don't travel, wanted to see them. The overland truck is the cheapest option as we camp and cook our own food for the group. As a result, this was a 'strange' group especially the grandmother from Wigan.

On our third night travelling through Uganda, we stopped at a beautiful camp site, where Bill Gates had stayed. The campsite was full of trees and bushes and a large swimming pool. The bar was a huge tent with a very large fire in the centre. We were on the Equator in Africa, but we were 2,000 metres above sea level, so the nights were cold.

Most of us went to the bar and had a few drinks in front of the fire. At around 10pm we all went to bed leaving the 'rough' woman from Wigan behind. Basically, she was aged 60 with 10 grandchildren but wore a mini skirt that was unsuitable as she was overweight, loud and horrible. You have probably guessed I didn't like her!!!

At 1am I had a knock on my tent, "Mike I need your help", it was Tim the black African trip leader, a nice bloke who had a posh background, his father was a General in the Kenyan army. We got on very well together swopping stories.

"That woman from Wigan was injured and I need your help as she is shouting and going mad"

I dragged myself out of bed to investigate.

She was sitting outside a cabin, surrounded by broken glass with blood running down her head, clearly not happy ranting and shouting. Her injury was self-inflicted. She had jumped out of the window—why? – no idea and she didn't know either. She was surrounded by African guards carrying old fashion rifles gawping at her.

I decided I need to take charge as Tim was flapping.

First, I got rid of all the guards. Then I asked her "What had happened?" – basically, she told me to "f**k off" and that "I can look after myself".

Tim, the trip leader told me he HAD to take her to hospital for insurance purposes because of the cut head and that if anything went wrong, he would lose his job. I suggested to her we all go to hospital, again she told me to "f**k off" and started to shout and rant.

RIGHT, I had enough, and I need to assert my authority.

I aggressively shouted at her to "F**king shut up as we are going to hospital NOW", she went very quiet and agreed. But there was no taxi as the nearest town was miles away. So, the camp manager drove us, the car must have been at least 20 years old and very battered. We set off to the nearest town, but the stupid woman started to rant and rave, again I shouted aggressively at her to make sure she didn't do anything stupid, like jump out of the car whilst it was moving.

In the middle of nowhere we ran out of petrol, it was pitch black.

We were close to a top of a hill, so after pushing the car to the top we then 'free wheeled down the hill' – not the cleverest thing to do in Africa – at the bottom we found a petrol station and woke up the owner who lived above it to fill up. This would never have happened in England.

A few minutes later we were at the hospital, again I had to shout at her to stop complaining and just let the Dr help her. She needed 6 stitches as the wound was deep.

I got back to the tent at 4am and then at 5am the alarm went off!!

What had happened? Basically, she got drunk – and then she lost it – shouting and swearing and then started throwing bottles against the wall. She got back to the cabin (she had upgraded from camping) smashed the window and then decided to jump out of the window and as a result cut her head open.

For the rest of the trip – she never spoke to me or even said thank you.

13

Gorillas – hiking in the impenetrable forest

Bwindi Impenetrable Forest – a UNESCO World Heritage site

To get to the Gorillas you first must find them which means hiking through the impenetrable forest. The forest trackers know roughly where they are, they locate them most days and follow them through their territory in the forest. The key is to know where they have slept the night before and then track them from there. This means, of course, you need to be deep in the forest just after dawn, so you start hiking predawn.

If you are an experienced tracker, it is relatively easy to follow them as they bulldoze their way through the forest eating what they want and breaking branches etc. However, finding the general area they slept in can mean walking up to 5 hours to find them and then 5 hours back. We were lucky we only had to walk for 2 hours through the forest – **except you don't walk, you battle.** The forest covers steep hills and ravines, and the undergrowth is thick bushes, nettles and lots of thorn plants which catch on your clothes. We all were given a strong stick to help keep our balance to prevent us falling into the gullies.

There were 6 of us and 2 trackers who had machetes and literally cut a path through – we fell, climbed over fallen trees, crossed steams that were three metres wide and half a metre deep, climbed steep muddy banks – bloody hard work. We were also lucky that we came across a wild Elephant track which made it slightly easier as they had bulldozed a path through. 2 hours was hard but doable BUT 5 hours would have been very hard, and a lot of visitors would have struggled to make it.

The woman from Wigan (see chapter, Violent Grandmother from Wigan) was in another group, on a different day, lucky for her they

43

only had to walk 25 minutes on a fairly open track, even so it took three local helpers, which you can hire, to push and shove her there.

Watching Gorillas

My first view of the Gorillas was a young one climbing through the branches of a tree, a black hairy beast with leaves and sticks stuck to the fur, an animal of the forest. The Gorilla pack was on the move, feeding and moving, trying to keep up in the forest was fun.

We were allowed 1 hour with them and then that is it for the day, no more visitors until the next day. It is very well managed and controlled. It takes approximately 2 years before a gorilla pack will get accustomed to the trackers and allow visitors to approach.

During the 1 hour stay, I had many great views, and one animal was so close you could study his fingers, almost human like.

I was also very close to the silver back male who sat two metres from me behind a large bush, the view was poor, but you could sense and hear his presence. When he stood up and walked away, he was huge, and I had a great view of his full body before he disappeared in the undergrowth.

With adult Gorillas, particularly the males, you must avoid eye contact as 'full eye contact' is a sign of aggression. Several times I was 'face to face' with the dominant silver back male, sometimes less than three metres away, and both of us were constantly looking down whilst occasionally glancing upwards.

There were 12 Gorillas in the pack with one Silver Back as well as few younger males, however, the majority were females with youngsters ranging from 3 months to 3 years.

It was a great experience seeing a dominant animal being comfortable in its natural environment.

14

Chance to fish in unusual places

Piranha fishing in the Pantanal

When I visited the Pantanal in Brazil, I knew that we would be staying next to a large river for 5 nights, so I packed my fishing rod on the off chance of being able to fish for a few hours. We went wildlife spotting from dawn till lunchtime and then late afternoon and evening to midnight, in between times most people went to bed BUT I went fishing. I packed a small spinning rod much to the amusement of my fellow wildlife travellers and fished for a couple of hours every day, catching a few small ones.

On the third day I caught 4 decent size Piranha with very large teeth compared to their size. The local chef heard about me fishing and suggested that if I catch anything decent, he will cook it for me. Piranhas have many small bones so the only way to eat it, is by making it into soup and straining out the small bones. So, that night I ate Piranha soup which was excellent – of course, I am bound to say that!!

Swakopmund Namibia and my SHARKS

Back in England I read about shark fishing from the beach in Namibia so I had to give it a go – my dad who taught me to fish would have been proud.

I was travelling from South Africa to Uganda on an overland truck for 3 months and during this trip we stayed in Swakopmund, Namibia, for a couple of days. I found a fisherman via the internet in Swakopmund who agreed to take me fishing, for a fee.

We drove to a deserted beach, 60 miles north of Swakopmund and once we had left town, we met no one on a dirt track next to the beach that stretched for hundreds of miles. This is the famous

Skeleton Coast where, in the past, hundreds of ships were wrecked because of the thick fog that can occur on this coast due to the meeting of cold sea water and hot air from the desert. Due to modern technology the last shipwreck was in the 1960s.

I had the whole beach to myself – miles each way and behind the beach, just desert – real wilderness fishing.

Overall, I caught 4 sharks and several smaller fish. The biggest a 70lb Six Gilled Shark.

- One 5lb Tope
- One 50lb Cow shark
- One 50lb Six Gilled shark
- One 70lb Six Gilled shark

The 70lb shark gave the best fishing fight I have ever had, pulling the line off the reel and pulling me 60 metres down the beach. It took me 20 minutes to land it. Great fun – my dad would have loved it – catching sharks on a deserted beach in the middle of nowhere.

A great memory of Africa – truly great.

Fishing a lagoon at night in the Maldives

I was on a whale watching boat trip sailing the Maldives archipelago which stretches over 1,000 miles. We anchored up one night in a huge lagoon that covered eight by ten miles and the captain asked if I would like to go fishing, of course, I said yes.

So, the captain, another crew member and I went out on a small boat and sailed two miles from the main boat into the middle of the lagoon. We dropped our hand lines into the water, turned out all lights and just drifted, in silence and darkness, under the moon and stars. You could not see land and the only light was the main boat at anchor, we just drifted along catching fish between two and six lbs, which we had for dinner the next night.

Fishing in Milford Sound, New Zealand – a near death experience

Sarah and I had booked a six night boat trip through Fiordland visiting several fiords in a very isolated part of the world. It was a luxury boat trip, to keep Sarah happy as she doesn't like boats, sleeping 20 passengers and with a top chef who used to cook for Richard Branson.

First, we flew in, by helicopter, over the mountains and ridges of Fiordland with great views as the sun was out. We landed on the deck of the boat in a beautiful, isolated fiord with stunning weather. Unfortunately, that was the end of the nice weather and it rained and rained for the next 6 days with strong winds and rough seas. Sarah hated it, her worst nightmare.

However, I LOVED IT and went fishing every day. The fishing was not great, but the scenery and the environment were excellent.

I was the only passenger interested in fishing, so a boat hand called Pedro from Mexico and I fished from a small boat in the various fiords. We fished the mouth of Milford Sound which is actually a fiord, created by ice and glacier activity, however, for some reason the early settlers called it a 'sound' and it has stuck.

Fishing was good I caught several Blue Cod to three lbs and two small sharks up to one metre long. I also hooked a larger Blue Cod and when it came close to the surface I felt a short sharp tug – when I pulled it in only the Blue Cod head was left – a large shark had bitten off the body with ease.

Whilst we were fishing the wind significantly increased and we decided to head to the main boat about 15 miles down the Sound where it was in a safe anchorage. Five miles down the Sound on the way back the wind direction changed and came from the land straight down the Sound as well as increasing in strength. Milford Sound is famous for having huge vertical cliffs, up to 1,500 metres, straight from the sea and hundreds of waterfalls especially when it had been raining. The waterfalls were 'full on' pouring water from the mountain tops.

The strong winds started to bounce off the cliff sides and circulate in the Sound. As the wind strength increased there were frequent whirlwinds with funnel shapes moving across the water, as a result we slowed down to five miles an hour. The winds were so strong some of the waterfalls were flowing uphill being blown up by the winds.

We came to a narrow section of the Sound with particularly high cliffs which generated many whirlwinds and one particularly large one came straight at us, a large vortex of whirling wind and water picked up from the surface of the sea.

Pedro, cut the speed down to one mile an hour and let go of the steering wheel, you can't fight this, we both just watched it come at us. When the vortex hit us, it ripped around the boat and lifted us slightly out of the water turning us 90 degrees. The boat was c8 metres long and made of steel, everything was steel so very solid and heavy however, the wind just picked us up and turned us as easy as anything.

We just looked at each other and laughed nervously and headed home very slowly.

Pedro told me afterwards he was 'very scared' however, I had confidence in him being a good sailor. I was also 'banking' on that there were other larger boats in the sound, and we would have been seen and rescued, hopefully!!!.

Catching a GT

I love watching, the Extreme Fishing TV programme presented by Robson Green.

I knew there were large number of sporting fish in the tropics, but I assumed you must be wealthy to fish for them. However, after watching Extreme Fishing I realised that in the right areas the infrastructure exists, and you can fish within my budget. Also, there are sport fish in the 10 to 100lb group which are more accessible, and you don't need large fishing boats (and money).

I really wanted to catch medium size sport fish in the Tropics especially a GT – a Giant Trevally.

Once I had booked the whale watching trip in the Maldives, I started to research fishing trips and found a boat that would take me out for six hours for £500, expensive but 'you only live once'. I decided to stay on for 5 nights in the Maldives after the whale watching trip had finished and booked a stay on an island 10 miles from the capital, where the fishing boat was based, so that I could also go scuba diving as well as fishing.

The fishing boat picked me up at 7am and for nearly 1 hour we travelled at high speed into the ocean – best fishing is away from the main island. The boat was owned and managed by an old experienced local man and his son (aged mid 30's). When asked; "What do I wanted to do with the fish – keep them? Return them?" – I replied "no, you can keep them" (I thought that would do for their tip).

They looked at each other, grinned and nodded – I didn't realise at the time, but it was a brilliant answer – as we stayed out for 11 hours all for the price of 6. Basically, they used the extra time to catch fish for the market and make themselves some additional money.

Where did we fish?

On the edge of a large reef surround by the Indian ocean with no land in sight. We fished either on top of the reef or in the deep channels running alongside it.

Was it good? Bloody hot and hard work, but great fun. We were out in the full sun all day – I thought I would get sunstroke.

But did we catch?

Well, they did – between them they caught 18 fish, all decent size between 10 and 30lbs – I just caught the sun!!

For most of the day I didn't catch anything and then caught a 3lb snapper, smallest fish of the day, and then a Groper.

BUT THEN – just before we finished, I felt as though I had caught a rock – nothing moved except I was fishing at the surface.

I kept the pressure on the rod and still nothing moved – for up to 5 minutes. It then dived and swam strongly away – and then up and around. The fight took at least 10 to 15 minutes, eventually it tired and I brought it to the net.

Biggest fish of the day 40lb Giant Trevally, often called GT.

It made my day – week and year – Robson Green eat your heart out – watching Extreme Fishing gave me the belief and idea that opportunities like this exist – I had wrongly assumed you must spend thousands to be able to do it.

Guinea Bissau – full week sports fishing

I had got the bug and wanted to go on a 'proper sports fishing' holiday.

Guinea Bissau is in West Africa 7 degrees north of the equator and was known as 'white man's grave' as around 100 years ago we didn't have the appropriate medicine or any natural resistance to the tropical diseases.

We fished in Orango Pargue National Park.

This national park is made up of hundreds of sand islands ranging from small (100 by 200 metres) to many large islands, largest being 20 miles by 15 miles with virgin tropical forests. The islands were beautiful .... white sand surrounding the island whilst the centre was covered with forest with huge trees which looked like primary forest c300 to 500 years old.

The sand islands were formed by a combination of a delta from several medium sized rivers (very large compared to the UK but small when you compared to major rivers around the world) and the shape of the coast. Guinea Bissau is a large inlet in the overall continental shape so the Atlantic Ocean forms huge eddies when the tide runs depositing floating material especially sand. Over the whole area the water is shallow with the maximum depths of 70 metres but mainly 5 to 30 metres but there are also deep channels with fast currents.

The undulating seabed with massive areas of sand banks, holes and channels form an excellent breeding area for 'bait fish', they have a name, but we just called them 'bait fish'. As a result, this attracts large number of predators, fish, such as 'Jacks' and Barracuda and a significant number of Dolphins, we saw reasonable numbers of Bottlenose, Risso, Common and Long Snouted Spinner.

The fishing is very good because the traditional tribes in this area look to the forest for food and survival and ignore the coast unlike surrounding countries such as Senegal and Gambia which have a fishing culture as a result these areas are very heavily over fished.

A small tribe called the Bijago people lived in the National Park and as a tribe it is run by women. Bijago people live with nature taking only what the need to live and their religion is based on the 'spirits from the animals'.

Women are the bosses they;

- Choose their husband.
- Decide if they are going to get divorced.
- Own and build their house.
- Organise labour for the husband and children as well as running the household.

I met a few local people going about their daily lives, a 'hunter gathering' lifestyle almost 'stone age', for example;

- Ladies and children collecting 'molluscs and shellfish' at low water.
- Men fishing from the shore with only a small 'cast net'.
- Men moving between island in 'wooden canoes' with only a paddle.
- Men climbing palm trees by rope around their waist to gain the fruit.

Hotel – very small and rustic .... loved it.

It was 50 metres from the beach, through woodland, up to a small hotel with room for only 12 guests, when I stayed there were only 4 of us (all fishing). Bedrooms were in individual huts scattered around the area, very basic but relatively clean .... sometimes hot running water sometimes not. Electricity fails every day, often failing for several hours at a time especially at night. When the electricity goes off, the fans go off and the room temperatures soars and wakes you up ...full of sweat.

But it is rural Africa.

And the room was full of wildlife, bugs, geckos and a very large millipede (300mm long).

The centre of the hotel had a long veranda about 30 metres long with a bar at one end and dining tables at the other. This was wonderful, an open veranda with a large, thatched roof, looking out through the trees to the ocean. Every night we had pre-dinner beers and then dinner on the veranda. Bats, dozens of them, would fly within the veranda, below the roof, catching bugs and during the day these would be replaced with swallows. These would often fly inches above our heads while we were eating.

We also had a 'pet vulture' that would sit just outside the veranda on the small trees as well as hopping on the ground, it was not a pet, just got very confident around humans. It would sit on a small tree just next to the entrance to the dining area waiting for one of us to keel over, it was a great advert for dinner!!!

Best Fishing – Chimneys

This was the best fishing location and has featured on 'Extreme fishing' TV programme staring Robson Green, loved by my nephew Alistair and myself.

This was 16 miles offshore and is known as Chimneys. It is a wreck of a cargo ship that sank in 12m of water, I believe the wreck to be c70 years old but it's uncertain and difficult to get accurate information. The ship settled upright on the bottom and the chimneys protrude straight up out of the water. The ship was clearly well-built as the chimney block was solid. This part of the Atlantic Ocean is relatively sheltered and doesn't suffer from rough weather so given the age of the wreck there is relatively little damage.

We fished all around the wreck and quickly worked out that one side of it was a sand bank and on the other a deep hole, obviously caused by the current.

Fishing was excellent with many bites, and we caught loads..... Snappers, Jacks, Barracudas and others

It was our favourite place, and we went twice.

Swarming Jacks chasing 'bait fish' on the surface

This was an amazing sight.... thousands of Jacks (from 10lb to 50lbs) bunched together chasing bait fish on the surface .... the water exploded in a dense patch of c40 by 40 metres with thousands of Jacks bunched together.

They would appear by magic and then disappear, moving in all directions.

We saw this around 30 times at the Chimneys in the surrounding water, however, the Ocean is still a big place, and they rarely came close. But we were lucky as twice they came within castings distance of the boat. We had an extra rod set up to fish on the surface if they came close. Normally we would be fishing on the bottom but if the Jacks were on the surface we quickly changed to the spare rod.

Fishing this way is great fun BUT hugely frustrating as most of the time the fish are out of reach. You could chase them, in the boat, but this is next to impossible as they appear quickly and then disappear.

The first time they came relatively close to the boat we had waited and waited for c10 minutes as they were too far out and then they turned and came straight towards us. My first and only cast (you only get one chance) hit the swarm in the middle and straight away BANG …. fish on.

On a light spinning rod the fight was great …. long runs and heavily bent rod.

Brilliant …. hard fighting fish….. a 25lb Jack…. my first of the trip….. brilliant…. brilliant.

Large Cobia Fish

My first Cobia hit my bait like a rocket and pulled my rod down so violently and strongly it pulled me double, I held on tight to the boat so as not to be pulled overboard. I remember shouting out 'f**king hell' in surprise as I held on.

I have never felt a bite like it.

Luckily the fish was well hooked and fought strongly …. it came to the boat 3 times but every time it saw the boat it got a second wind and swam off stripping metres and metres of line. Eventually after around 30 minutes it was in the boat….. 125lb fish….my biggest ever fish …. lovely.

Cobia is a tropical sport fish that hunt fish but also squid in the top and medium layers of the water, but they don't have huge teeth, more likely to suck in their food and pick off injured fish etc. They have a reputation of following sharks to pick off scraps during a feeding frenzy. However, they are a strongly built fish and fight extremely hard. It also one of the best tasting fish in the area and is very expensive in the local market...much sort after.

We ate my fish that night and quickly understood why it had such a good reputation.

15

8 : 3

Background

On my overland trip through Africa, we were crossing the border between Malawi and Tanzania. These crossings always take time and can take hours with lots of paper checking and bureaucracy. Once the truck was in the queue I got out for a walk whilst keeping an eye of the truck for progress.

I met a young lad, aged 12, selling bananas. I said, no to the bananas and asked what football team he supported, a great ice breaker in Africa.

Arsenal, he replied with a grin.

"NO – follow a great team like Man Utd" I cried.

Two weeks ago, Man Utd beat Arsenal 8 : 3 so I held up 8 fingers and repeated the score.

We chatted for c20 minutes covering football, school subjects and because he was a clever lad who spoke excellent English we touched on world politics – he had a good understanding of world issues for a young lad. I was very impressed. But every now again I would go back to raising 8 fingers with a grin he would reply with 3 fingers.

I noticed our driver heading back up the queue, so it was time to go. I offered the lad £5, in local money, to help him out – he then held out the bananas which I refused with a shake of my head, "You keep" I said.

"Only take the money if you take the bananas" he firmly stated

"Ok" – handing over the cash with a shrug. I asked, "What are you going to do with the cash?"

"Watch football" he replied.

"Is a there a local game on?" I enquired.

He looked at me if I was stupid "Liverpool Chelsea are playing this afternoon". I looked around …we were in the middle of nowhere … no villages …no power lines…nothing.

"How? Where do you live?"

"My village is 3 miles over there and the Chief has a tele"

"Ahh you are the Chief's son?" I enquired

"No" again looking at me if I was stupid.

"Explain?"

"Chief has a TV, generator and internet disc so he can get the football and we pay the Chief to watch the game"

"How many will be watching?" I asked think about 10

"Oh, it could be a good game, should be around 300".

At this point I need to go, so bid my farewells and walked back to the truck. On the way back I turned and with a grin held up 8 fingers. And with a bigger grin he held up 3.

Premier league football gets everywhere

Sad part of the Man Utd v Arsenal 8 : 3 Result

Sam the driver of the 2nd stage of the overland African trip (see Witchcraft charter) told me about the result and as part of the discussion he told me that after the game there was a largescale riot, in Nairobi, between the two different supporters.

Basically, different tribes in Kenya support different Premier league clubs, only the top teams, of course. As a result of the riot 8 people were killed – over a game that had taken place 4,300 miles away. However, he did say they only need an excuse to riot against each other.

Maldives

After my whale watching trip, I stayed for 5 days on an island close to the main island and the capital, roughly 10 miles away. The idea was I could go scuba diving, but also wanted to go on a professional sports fishing trip in the tropics, similar to the 'Extreme Fishing' TV programme that I love. I had prebooked a boat, from the UK, for 6 hours, it was expensive, but it was a 'dream trip'. The boat picked me up at 7am, from my island, and was skippered by an old man. His crew was his young son, aged c30. See 'chapter 'Chance to fish in unusual places'

The fishing trip was excellent, fishing remote reefs and deep channels, but it was hot and hard work. Unfortunately, I only caught 3 fish whilst they caught 18 between them, all a decent size. However, I did catch a GT or Giant Trevally weighting 40 lbs, it was the fish I wanted to catch – I was delighted.

Having been on the water for 5 hours the skipper said we go for lunch during the 'heat of the day', so we motored to a small island that had a café. The island had a small village, small harbour and café whose customers were small commercial fishing boats that followed the migrating fish shoals as well as passing commercial boats going to the main island to sell or pick up goods. There was no tourist village on the island.

The food was good, basic but good, the menu, however, was limited to two dishes. After the meal I asked if I could go to the loo, via the skipper as only he spoke English.

"Sorry, no toilet" the manager of the café replied. After a short discussion, in their native language, the manager took me to his home to visit his toilet, only a short distance away.

I entered a large room with two pieces of furniture:

- A large settee with a young boy resting on it.
- And the largest TV I have ever seen covering the wall

AND, being shown on the TV was 'Chelsea v Norwich' football match.

I could not believe it. In the middle of the Indian Ocean on a remote island in the Maldives the young lad was watching English Premier League Football.

16

Being hunted by a large Nile Crocodile

Background

On my overland trip though Africa we stayed at Victoria falls for four nights. Above the Victoria Falls is the Zambezi River, a large mature river approximately one mile across and shallow next to flat open woodland. It then hits a large fault in the underlying rock and as a result a large gorge has been created by the Victoria Falls. The waterfall is one mile wide at the height of the wet season and plunges c115metres.

After the fall the canyon is called Batoka Gorge which stretches for 70 miles. Compared to the river above Victoria falls the gorge is narrow 1/3 mile wide and the river runs fast, having both deep parts and shallows with impressive rapids. The sides of the gorge are around 800 metres tall and raise vertically from the water, very spectacular.

White water rafting in the Batoka gorge is world famous and is grade level 5 which is the highest non-professionals are allowed to do. So, I booked an all-day trip.

Crocodile hunt

Throughout the day we rafted 30 miles and between rapids there were often large stretches of open deep water. During these periods we could jump in, wearing our life jackets, floating in the fast current. I thought this was wonderful floating along looking at the scenery, the huge cliffs and watching the birds.

Most people did it for a short period and then got back into the raft. But I loved it and towards the end I was the only person in the water. At one point I had drifted c600 metres in front of the raft, further down was a safety kayak about 300 metres away. I felt perfectly safe.

Suddenly the kayak paddler became very alert and signalled, a triangle with his arms and then paddled furiously towards me. A quick look around and the raft was also going 'full pelt' again straight at me.

"Oh my god, that must be a croc" I thought.

I tried to keep still as much as possible as crocodiles are attracted to animals splashing around in the water.

"What is going on?" I enquired when the kayak reached me.

"Oh nothing" he shrugged

"Come on, it is croc?"

"Just keep still and hang onto the kayak" nodding in agreement.

Trying to keep your legs still whilst being dragged along at full speed, by the kayak, whilst in a fast current, is impossible. Soon the raft arrived, and the skipper lifted me straight into it, no messing around. After catching my breath and calming down I asked the group leader from my overland trip, who happened to be on the raft (he gets a free trip).

"Go on tell me the truth, was it a large croc?" I asked.

'Yes, probably 3 to 4 metres" he replied.

"In hunting mode?"

"Oh yes, full hunting mode"

"I thought so, I put my chances of being taken at 1 in 5, what do you think?" I enquired

"Actually, I had it as 1 in 4, it was in full hunting mode" he replied with a grin.

Surprisingly I was calm as the danger had passed.

"So, what are they going to do now, you can't have a large croc around with all these travellers?"

"Yes, I talked to the skipper (who he knew well) it must have come upriver in the last few days, and they will shoot it tonight. It is too risky to have around and, if they don't get it tonight, they will have to close the rafting down until they do"

Rafting

I have rafted a couple of times before and enjoyed it.

I managed to get the front spot, it's the best spot as you get the full impact. Over the 30 miles there are 22 rapids ranging from grade three to five. We had gone through six or seven rapids hitting some big waves and losing several people overboard, but we had kept the raft up right.

We then hit a grade four which was a decent size but not the biggest but at the wrong angle as soon as we hit it. We hit a vertical wall of water that flipped us straight up and over backwards. I was clinging on but was tossed through the air backwards.

I can clearly remember plunging deep under water, with the sunlight through what appeared still water, a lovely sight. I was relaxed as I knew my life jacket would 'kick in' and then I would float to the surface.

I was beginning to run out of breath BUT as soon as I surfaced, I was hit by another massive wall of water which smashed into me pushing me deep under water without having a chance to get a breath. It happened again and I was getting scared as I was very short of air. However, on the fourth attempt I manged to grab some air and after a few minutes I swim towards the raft.

After that we went down many large rapids but managed to keep the raft upright, but only just on some occasions. Osten, my Swedish friend, who was on my raft, went in three times and when we stopped for lunch his hands were badly shaking. "Are you cold" I asked.

"NO terrified".

Victoria Falls

I had planned my trip through Africa to coincide with the dry season so providing better wildlife viewing opportunities. We arrived at Victoria Falls, in the dry season, even so it was spectacular. Of course, in the wet you can't get close to the falls and white-water rafting is only available in the dry season.

The river has exploited a fault in the rocks and as a result has worn out a large gulley that is a mile long which now forms Victoria Falls. At the far end of the gulley is the lowest point of the falls, c100 metres high, so the river is concentrated here, and the waterfall is spectacular. Further along the gulley the falls are completely dry, at this time of the year. I thought the combination of large volume of water concentrated in one section and dry cliffs was excellent as I could understand the geography of the place.

To get to the falls, which is on the borders of Zambia and Zimbabwe, you cross the large road and railway bridge that is often shown in photographs in the newspapers. On the way back we stopped to watch a couple of bungee jumpers – daft buggers.

17

Covered in Whale Snot and
being interviewed on Radio 4

Over the recent years I have seen large number of whales and
dolphins covering a wide variety of species. However, I had not seen
a whale until my Antarctic trip prior to my 40th birthday.

Up close and personal

During my Antarctic trip I saw over 150 different whales, mainly
Humpbacks, and had many good views. Unfortunately, these were
all from the ship so by definition you are not going to get too close.

What I wanted was a 'close encounter' to really see and experience
the animal.

In total, the ship carried 70 passengers however we were a separate
group on a dedicated wildlife trip (15 of us) with our own leader,
Mark Carwardine, who has since become a famous TV and radio
wildlife personality. After several days of watching whales, from a
distance, I asked and nagged him if we could go out in the zodiacs to
see if we could get closer to the whales. After a while he realised,
I was dedicated wildlife watcher being on deck between 6am and
10pm everyday (I loved it) and even though I say it myself, I am
good at spotting whales and took my time to ensure others got to see
them which impressed him.

Towards the end of the trip, I finally got my wish.

The ship stopped 20 miles from mainland Antarctica in the middle
of the Antarctic Ocean where the currents are circulating due to a
huge underwater rock formation. The circulating water traps
icebergs but also attracts whales due to the abundance of feed. The
zodiacs were split into two groups, the other passengers went to

look at the icebergs whilst our group (eight passengers to a zodiac) headed off to try and find whales.

We set off, at speed, in a snowstorm with visibility around 800 metres and a small sea swell. After 15 minutes the snowstorm increased, visibility dropped to 100 metres and the swell increased to one metre. I was beginning to think 'what have I done', we are in the middle of the ocean, no idea where the ship is, can't see a thing and what happens if the zodiac is flipped over. And it is my daft idea!!!

Lucky the visibility rapidly improved and there to the right, 800 metres away, I spotted a 'blow' I had found a Humpback Whale. We headed over in that direction and cut the motor.

After a few minutes it surfaced about 100 metres away and then proceed to swim, underwater, around the zodiac coming up for air every five minutes whilst getting closer and closer to the boat. It disappeared and then I saw a huge underwater shape coming slowly up straight underneath the zodiac. As it got closer it slowed down and the front of the whale came out the water less than a metre from me.

If I had leaned out, I could have touched it, of course, I didn't as I could have spooked it.

After a few minutes it went under and then reappeared about 10 metres away this time it rose five metres out of the water, and you could see his big black eye looking at us. It then swam towards the Zodiac and as it came close it 'blew' – I and the others were covered in spray and slim, whale snot, it covered our clothes, hair and face – marvellous.

I had got my close and personal encounter with a whale – I was delighted.

My Radio 4 interview by Mark Carwardine

Mark had a short weekly wildlife slot on Radio 4 and asked if I would be happy to be interviewed. Why not. I had the star slot and had 6 minutes of fame with an estimated audience of ¾ million.

Killer Whale or Orca

I have also had the pleasure of being covered in Orca snot whilst watching a large male and two females off the coast of Vancouver Island Canada. The Orca drifted closed to the small boat we were on and blew heavily covering us is spray and Orca snot.

Blue Whales

I had a great encounter with a large female Blue Whale with her calf off Mexico in the Pacific Ocean.

Usually when watching a swimming whale, you see 1/3, 1/3 and then 1/3, i.e., you see the head above water and then as the bodies comes up the head goes down under water and then finally you see the tail. On this occasion, after following her for over an hour, she slowed down and stretched out in full. You could see her whole body, at that point you fully realise how big she was, yet sleek and streamlined. She was a big female and the skipper estimated that she was 30 metres long.

The water was particularly clear, and the sun was in the right direction, so you see how blue she was, and I realised for the first time why they are called Blue Whales as before they have always looked dark.

Breaching

One of the greatest wildlife spectacles is to watch great whales breaching.

I been lucky to see it a few times and it is great experience. Watching a 50-ton Humpback Whale come out of the water and then the huge splash of water as it lands.

Most of the time a whale doesn't jump clear of the water it leaves its tail in the water. However, in Antarctica I saw a large Humpback jump completely out of the water, on several occasions. Unfortunately, my camera was playing up and I didn't manage to record the event.

18

How the Elephant found a lost
wallet in a huge floodplain

Background

I visited Kaziranga National Park in Assam India to see Great One Horn Indian Rhinos.

The park is huge, 25 mile long and eight miles wide, and lies in the flood plain of the Brahmaputra River, one of the great rivers of the world. In the wet season the river in this area can be 200 miles wide and yet, in the dry season, only 10 miles. The park is a vast expanse of tall elephant grass, up to five metres high, grass flood plains, forest areas and huge number of lagoons. It is famous for its Rhino with a population, in 2022, of 2,400 out of a world population of 3,700. It also has Indian Elephant, wild water Buffalo, the rare Barasingha deer and a healthy population of Tigers (c100).

The group I was with had five full days exploring the various habitats mostly by jeep but also on elephant back looking for Rhinos. You sat on the elephant back legs wide part like riding a horse, which was great fun as you cling on as the elephant goes up and down six metre banks, wading through rivers and walking through the tall elephant grass creeping up on the Rhinos.

Missing wallet

On the second Elephant trip we were on a mission to find a rare bird called Swamp Francolin. They live on the floodplains which are huge, the one we decided to explore was approximately five miles by two. There were five Elephants in our group, and we split up in a search pattern across the grass plain, the grass being a foot high. We wandered randomly across the floodplain, changing directions, many times, to try and locate the birds. Eventually we found them, a nice bird, with a world population of c10,000, so rare. After finding the birds we headed to the wetter part of the reserve with tall elephant grass to view Rhinos. Overall, the trip was 90 minutes.

On arriving back at the Elephants base camp our group leader realised he had lost his wallet whilst riding the Elephants as he remembered checking it before we left. The Elephant Mahouts (driver) on hearing this said they would find it.

I was thinking NO CHANCE as we didn't follow any set footpaths just wandered around trying to locate the bird in a huge floodplain. Overall, we must have covered at least six miles over a 90-minute period. However, they were adamant they would find it. All they need was for each Elephant to have a sniff of his clothes. They then set off very determined to find the wallet, you could see the competition between the Mahouts.

NO CHANCE

Instead of waiting around we set off on a jeep safari and came back after 2 hours. To my utter astonishment they had found the wallet, it took only 20 minutes. The Mahouts were full of pride and 'pleased as punch'. We gave them all a large tip.

It was an exceptional piece of animal skill. The Elephants had remembered the smell of the leader and then locating the wallet, by smell, in deep grass in a relatively short period.

Drinking tea with an Army General surrounded by heavily armed guards and 4 machine gun posts.

Kaziranga National Park is in Assam, in Northeast India, approximately eight hours drive from the capital. The journey was through open countryside with small villages. Assam looks significantly richer than central India, where I had been before, but it's still a third world country. Assam and particularly further east from where we were going had significant internal problems with communist rebels.

On the journey to the park, we stopped at a tea house in open countryside, it was very pleasant sitting outside having lunch.

An army convoy arrived with four lorries and a staff car in between the lorries, the leading one had a machine gun on top of the cab. Very quickly the lorries unload c70 soldiers who formed a large circle approximately 80 metres around the tea house and set up four machine gun posts.

Then, in the middle, a soldier set up a table with white tea cloth and started brewing tea beside the table. At this point a General strolled over from his staff car and sat down and had a cup of tea.

This all happened very quickly and efficiently. After his cup of tea, they quickly packed up and left – the whole event taking 10 minutes.

We sat there 'open mouthed'.

19

Sitting by a water hole drinking beer

Background

If you are planning an African safari, I would recommend having a night stop next to a watering hole especially in the dry season. We camped close to a watering hole in Etosha National Park.

Luckily the viewing area was on a large, raised bank and immediately below us was a large double fence but was not intrusive as we looked over it. The nearest edge of the water was 40 metres away, overall, the water hole was relatively small due to dry season, being no more than 100 metres by 50 metres with a spring which you could see bubbling away.

My trip buddy, Osten, and I found a quiet spot, sat and watched, as well as drinking a few beers, from 7pm to 1am, we would have stayed up all night, but we had a 6am safari in the morning. It was relatively quiet to start with, a few Impalas and Zebras, and then the fun started.

First, a White Rhino appeared to be shortly joined by another. They kept their distance drinking and bathing in the water.

Then a Black rhino appeared.

They didn't like sharing. The water hole was big enough for two but not three. They looked at each other, snorted at each other, walked around each other, stopped had a drink. But when it was uncomfortably crowded, they mock charged each other. This went on for two hours, huffing and puffing with at least 30 mock charges and some of them close to us.

They were not happy. Great fun for us.

Around 10pm three elephants came in, one male, one female and a small baby. The baby was very small and wobbly on its feet so probably less than six months old. Elephants don't like to share their water and basically, they kicked out the Rhinos who disappeared as soon as they saw the elephants approaching. Without the Elephants the Rhinos looked huge but was dwarfed by the male Elephant which looked three times larger.

They dominated the water hole drinking and bathing for 30 minutes.

During this period three female lions appeared, in the distance, about 400 metres away and settled down to watch.

The female and baby Elephant started to move off, in the general direction of the lions, who became interested in the baby, standing and moving slowly towards it. Immediately the male Elephant charged the lions making them gallop away.

After the Elephants had gone two Rhinos appear, obviously waiting in the background for the Elephants to finish. They were followed by a female Rhino and baby. These Rhinos shared the water hole between them, very peaceful, drinking and bathing.

Lions re-appeared on the edge of the water hole, slumped in the same spot as before.

After an hour the female and baby moved off, again, in the general direction of the lions. Again, the lionesses perked up and moved to within 30 metres of the baby, as which point the mother became very alert and charged the lionesses making them scatter. As soon as they settled down, she charged again and again, moving them further away. I enjoyed the Lions being bullied, makes a nice change.

A good night with lots of interesting behaviours.

Lionesses did get their supper as when we set off on a safari, next day, we spotted them close to the water hole eating a Zebra.

20

How a dolphin nearly crashed into me

Background

As part of my overland trip through Africa, we stopped at Zanzibar Island, a wonderful place.

Six of us decided to go swimming with dolphins from a remote fishing village. The operation was run by local fishermen to earn a bit of extra cash rather than a 'slick' commercial outfit. The equipment was poor, the boat was old and rustic, no health or safety, basically you just got on with it.

We motored out into the Indian Ocean and after two miles I spotted a group of Bottlenose Dolphins. They seemed relaxed and hung around, so we dived in. The dolphins were curious and would come to have a look at us. If they didn't want to swim with us, they would just disappear into the ocean, they are in charge of the encounter. Basically, it is them looking at us, rather than us looking at them.

One of the techniques I learned in Mexico, is that once they are relaxed around you, if you splash, they will come in close to investigate. The others in the group thought this was funny but it works especially if you have the confidence of the animals. I have had many close encounters with Dolphins coming within two metres.

The Dolphins were moving around, feeding and socialising, so we were often in and out of the boat keeping up with them. On this particular occasion we had spread out and I could hear the Dolphins, below us, by their 'clicks' but could not see them in the gloom. Water visibility was excellent however they were at least 60 metres deep.

I decided to splash my flipper several times and then just lie dormant. There were two people either side of me, swimming around, but at least 20 metres away. Shortly after I splashed a Dolphin came out of the gloom heading straight towards the splash. As it rose from the deep, I laid motionless on the surface watching him approaching me.

As he got closer, he was on a direct trajectory to crash into me whilst I could see he was watching the other two who were moving around. As the Dolphin came even closer, c15 metres, I thought he had not seen me, I waited a bit longer then decided I must show myself as I wanted to avoid a collision.

So, I slowly moved my arms. At this point, he was three metres away and he came to a halt. His whole body twisted and shuddered and then stopped, finishing less than a metre away from my face. He looked straight at my face in astonishment and with puzzlement on his face, you could guess what he was thinking 'where the hell did you come from'!!!

We looked at each other 'face to face' for a couple of minutes. He then swam, several times, slowly around me staring at me before slowly moving away.

Overall, we swam with the pod for several hours, in and out of the boat following them around, then they decided they need to go fishing and disappeared. What was fantastic was listening to the Dolphins talking to each other – click, click, click – very loudly and clearly communicating to each other.

Galapagos Island

One morning at dawn, I spotted a couple of Dolphins several miles away by a few remote splashes. Overtime they gradually moved closer and closer, and the pod turned into a super pod, estimated at 1,500 Bottlenose Dolphins.

Once they approach the boat, they seemed very relaxed and hung around, so we decided to go and swim with them. We had c50 minutes in the water with them swimming around us coming to within three metres for a look but mostly five to ten metres away.

At one point when the Dolphins had disappeared, I had a quick look around, I was 500 metres from the boat, 2 miles from the shore, the water was c1,000 metres deep and when I looked down, I could not see further than 50 metres or so. I am in the Pacific Ocean, isolated in the water, I thought 'bloody hell, this is either good or mad!!'.

Other Dolphins

I have been very fortunate to swim with a few different species of dolphins such as Spotted and Spinner Dolphins in the Maldives as well as Dusky and Hector (smallest sea water dolphin) in New Zealand.

If you ever get the chance to swim with wild dolphins go for it.

Swimming with Penguins

Most people believe all Penguins come from Antarctica BUT it is not true, most do live on the edge of the Antarctic Circle, but large populations also live on countries such as, South Africa, New Zealand etc. However, the Galapagos Penguin lives and breeds on the equator and are endemic to Galapagos Island. There are only c5,000, so rare but doing ok.

The best bit was swimming with them, they swim like bullets so you can't keep up and they will avoid you, so the best chance is to wait in ambush and hope they swim in your direction. I was lucky, I was snorkelling along-side a rocky coastline with many small coves. I spotted 12 penguins that were just floating on the surface of the water. They had not seen me, so I slowly drifted motionless towards them, however, before I got close, they decided to move off going in different directions. They shot off like bullets and luckily four of them headed straight for me and quickly stopped less than a metre from my face. They all looked at me thinking 'what the bloody hell is that' and then shot off even quicker.

Sea Turtles

I have also had the pleasure of swimming with Sea Turtles, on numerous occasions, I love swimming with these graceful creatures.

They swim like the tortoise of the sea, slowly and relaxed without a care in the world. As a result, they are very approachable and often allowing you to swim next to them, sometimes less than a metre away, for many minutes and sometimes up to 30 minutes depending on how relaxed the turtle is.

Sea Snake – Two Band Sea Snake

I swam with several of these in Indonesia. It was excellent to watch them swimming around hunting in small holes searching for crabs and then every c15 minutes coming to the surface for air.

Sea snakes are very tame and curious so will come and look at you, except they are more deadly than any land snake. Their venom will kill you in minutes however, they will only bite if threatened.

Whilst watching one swim around, Ian, one of the passengers, got too close as the snake was swimming towards him. Ian was swimming in baggy shorts and at one point, unbeknown to him, the snake swam up his shorts – most entertaining.

Swimming with sharks

When you first see a shark underwater your heart naturally skips a beat even if it is only two metres long until you tell yourself – it is only a shark, which you repeat a few times. All the sharks I swam with have been relatively small one to three metres ranging from Nurse, Galapagos, reef sharks both Black and White tipped.

A great experience seeing them glide around.

In the Maldives I did manage to swim with a Whale Shark for five to ten minutes. We knew he was in the water swimming in our general direction as it was being followed by 2 swimmers and their boat signalled there was a Whale Shark below the surface.

I quickly dived in but had to swim 100 metres to get on the same line as the shark – all the time I was peering into the gloom thinking 'where are you'. Then he appeared swimming 10 metres below the surface at a reasonable pace – same as a human at a medium/fast pace.

By swimming at full speed, I managed to get above the shark and had a lovely view of the whole animal gracefully swimming along – he then slightly upped his pace and moved slightly deeper into the gloom. Of course, they can swim at least 10 times faster than us and was only cruising along.

Big Wrasse who attacked me – mock attack as a warning

Whilst swimming in the Maldives on a coral reef I found a huge Wrasse at least one metre long but also tall – must have weighed been between 60lb to 80lb, a powerful fish – with large teeth – at least 25 to 50mm long. Basically, it uses its teeth to break off coral and eat both the rock and the alga inside. The Wrasse then splits out the ground down rock whilst eating the alga.

I slowly approached it as it was eating – got within one metre and took many photos – some were excellent. After a while I could sense that he was getting agitated, and I was outstaying my welcome.

As I was moving away a big swell pushed me closer to him invading his body space. He launched an attack at me with those large teeth – but as the large swell push me around I lost sight of him. As I struggled with the swell, I was just a waiting for the bite, **thinking this is going hurt.**

As I managed to steady myself in the water, I saw that he had pulled out inches from my leg – luckily a mock attack as a warning.

Obviously, I got out of there as quickly as I could without provoking him further.

21

Weather in Antarctica – such extremes

We English love to talk about the weather however, the extremes in Antarctica are worth talking about.

Background

In January 1999, 5 months prior to my 40th birthday, I went on a trip to the Antarctic. I could now claim to have been to every continent before I was 40.

100 mile an hour wind

It was early morning, and we were slowly sailing close to the mainland in a deep channel. Clearly the skipper knew what was forecast as we were in lee of the mainland as the wind strength increased and increased. The winds were coming straight from the central ice cap, and it was very cold.

The ship was an ex-Russian spy/research vessel of 8,000 tons carrying c70 passengers. Above the bridge at the very top was a large viewing platform providing a 360-degree views of the surrounding sea. In the middle was a small box approximately five metres square and three metres tall with a radar mask. This viewing spot was my favourite place, and I was often joined by between 4 and 8 other passengers. It was very exposed so many people didn't like it.

As the winds increased and the cold intensified all other passengers started to move away to more sheltered areas or indoors. I was well dressed for the conditions having a warm vest, t shirt, thin jumper, a thick Aran jumper and a heavy Antarctic coat. On my face I had a full faced Balaclava, ski googles and a bobble hat. Because I was dressed for the occasion, I was relatively warm. My coat and

Balaclava were full of ice when I came downstairs people thought I looked like a snowman.

As the winds got stronger and stronger, I could not stand at the front of the viewing platform but sheltered on the leeward side of the radar box. Even though the winds were powerful many birds were flying around particularly Snow Petrels, a beautiful bird, that is seldom seen as they live deep in the Antarctic and nest on high cliffs on the ice cap.

That evening the captain of the ship informed us that the winds had, on several occasions, exceeded 100 miles an hour. Because we had sailed close to the mainland on the leeward side the sea was relatively calm.

Having been on the viewing platform for several hours I decided it was coffee and cake time and without thinking I moved towards the stairway and away from the shelter of the box. The wind caught hold of me and pushed me, very quickly, towards the railings which I was helpless to prevent. I quickly ducked down so all of my body was below the top of the railings and grabbed hold tightly so that it would not push me over the top.

Bracing myself against the railings, keeping my head down, I push hard and with much effort dragged myself along the railings towards the stairways battling the wind. When I got to the stairway, I laid on the ground and managed to edge myself over and down the stair which, being in a more sheltered spot, quickly became safe.

After coffee and 2 large slices of cake I moved to a more sheltered position.

Fascinating conditions – but scary.

Into the black unknown

The ship had anchored in a channel between a group of islands, and we had made a landing, for 2 hours, to view a Penguin colony. There had been no wind all morning and the seas were calm.

I was on the last Zodiac back to the boat when I spotted a couple of Humpback whales 800 metres away and on pointing it out to the driver, we made a detour away from the ship to have a closer look. The whales ignored us and floated around with the occasional shallow dive; it was nice to see. The Zodiac driver got a call on his ship radio requesting us to return immediately as the weather was changing. I looked around, it was still and calm with the sun out.... what!!

We headed straight back, unloaded, lifted the Zodiacs on board and set sail within 10 minutes. During this period, I changed my clothes, grabbed my gear, coffee and made my way up to my favourite spot on the viewing platform.

Sailing slowly down the channel I could see in the distance some dark clouds forming and as we approached, they turned into a thick black wall. Around the boat the sea was very calm with little wind but ½ mile away was this jet-black wall covering the sea and sky – it looked as though we were going to sail off the edge of the world.

In the space of a few minutes the weather changed abruptly to full on gale, with high winds, snowstorm with waves of around 3 metres. Inside the darkness we could see about 100 metres, yet, from the brightness on the other side it looked an impenetrable black wall. Talking to the crew they explained that this change of weather front is quite usual in the Antarctic. The distance between high and low-pressure fronts can be over very small distances.

Paradise Bay

Perfect name if the sun is shining.

We sailed into a large bay around mid-afternoon and dropped anchor. Paradise bay is a large bay surrounded by mountains up to 1,600 metres high covered in snow and glaciers. It is also relatively isolated from the sea so when there is little or no wind the sea is calm and flat.

We had perfect conditions. Blue sky, full sun, no wind with the sea being flat allowing the mountains to be reflected on the sea. The bay is full of ice floats and small icebergs with Penguins and Seals sitting on the ice.

We had a BBQ for dinner, and I sat outside in my T shirt watching the scenery and wildlife. I had my telescope on a Leopard seal, a huge creature maybe 3 metres long, these are one of the top predators in Antarctic and love eating penguins. As I was watching him on a small ice float a Penguin leapt out of the water landing within feet of the Leopard Seal. Almost at the same moment it jumped out of the water the Penguin jumped backwards reversing his movement, thinking, 'O my god'.

Nearly midnight sun

The Antarctic is a huge continent with the Peninsular, where most of the wildlife live and breed, outside the Antarctic circle. As a result, we didn't cross the Antarctic circle, but we did land on the continent many times.

The furthest south we reached was 64:49 degrees and by luck we anchored up for the night.

I decided to stay up to see how far the sun would go down and what the light conditions would be at midnight. Unfortunately, the sun set behind some distance mountains so didn't see the lowest point. Again, I was lucky as it was a calm clear evening and I enjoyed watching wildlife moving around I stayed up to 1am.

22

"Right, I am ready for a beer"

Background

A group of us who have known each other for over 40 years have an 'international lads' trip, roughly once a year. This trip was to Porto, Portugal where we stayed for 4 nights walking the city and having a glass of wine or two. There were seven of us on this trip.

We decided to have a day out to the Port grape growing area which was reached by a scenic rail journey lasting three hours. This was excellent, travelling alongside the major river that flows through to Porto with steep hillsides, on both sides, and the occasional traditional farmhouse.

We left the train at the village regarded as the centre of the port wine growing region. Given it was lunch time we wandered through the village avoiding the usual tourist cafes near the station and found a traditional café after 600 metres or so. We sat outside in the sun having a beer or wine and a sandwich.

"So, what's the plan?" someone asked. We agreed to go to a winery but wanted to avoid the large commercial ones advertised at the station, but which one?

Over lunch I noticed, straight across the valley, over a river, a medium size building that looked old but had clearly been done up. The old timber work looked great from this distance. I pointed it out and said "Why don't we try that one, it looks great, and is only a short walk down the valley, over the bridge and up the hill"

"Is it open as a winery?" someone enquired. "No idea, but it looks nice" I shrugged.

"We can always go for a nice walk and see what happens". I added.

We were in luck, the place had been recently restored, c3 years ago, and had been previously owned by the new owner's, grandad. There was a lot of pride in the place.

We booked a tour of the Port making factory and Port tasting, of course, we chose the most expensive option. The tour was good, and he gave a clear description of how Port is made, none of which I can remember now. Port tasting was in the old board room and was excellent. There was a huge, polished Oak table and wooden panelling on the wall, with old photographs. Nicely done up.

Tasting followed the usual pattern. Except he didn't put any of the open bottles away, so every time he got distracted or left the room, we quickly re-filled our glasses.

Towards the end Phil ask, "How do we go about buying some?"

"You can buy individual bottles".

"NO, I mean a crate, can you ship to England and what would that cost?" Phil asked.

"Yes, it depends on volume".

I replied, "I will have a few crates".

"And me," said Tim.

His eyes lit up and opened a few more bottles of Port and left the room. I love Port so I took advantage!!

Between us we ordered over £800 worth of Port including some brilliant White Port which I loved. And, because he got a good order, and we were genuinely interested in the business as well as having a friendly laugh between us he opened a few more bottles and left us helping ourselves to the Port.

After a while it was time to go. On getting outside I realised that I was drunk, very drunk. I remember thinking 'got to be sensible'.

Apparently, when we arrived at the station, I decided we all need some food, to help sober us up, and I took charge ordering burger and chips all round and negotiated that it would all be available before the train arrived. Afterwards the team said I was in total control and very lucid.

The train arrived and as it was very full most of us had to stand in the entrance area. I decided it was time for a kip. I walked halfway down the full carriage, laid down on the floor in the middle of the aisle and immediately fell asleep.

Including snoring very loudly.

After an hour the ticket inspector arrived – I opened one eye pointed to Phil and went back to sleep. I slept all the way back and woke up near Porto railway station.

I sat up – stretched and said to the team.

"Right, I am ready for a beer"

23

Twice as old as Jesus

Background

I love trees especially ancient woodlands that have never been cut down. There are natural, pure and provide a diversity of life. I have been lucky to experience many woodlands from the Amazon Rainforest to the Boreal Forests of the north.

There is one tree and woodland that had a lasting impression on me.

Baobab tree – Africa

Whilst travelling through the Kalahari Desert we camped at a lovely campsite with a bar and showers, which made a nice change. The campsite was in the middle of a Baobab woodland of several hundred trees. This part of the Kalahari is classified in habitat terms as semi desert, so the trees are often 50 to 100 metres apart, a very low-density woodland. To survive in this harsh environment, they have developed very long and deep root systems.

Baobabs are massive trees similar to the Sequoia tree from California, huge squat trunks often 10 to 12 metres wide with large boughs and branches. The bark is pale in colour and when caught in the setting sun are very photogenic.

I discovered the owner of the campsite was passionate about the trees and bribed him with several beers to tell me what he knew. He informed me that majority of the trees are at least 2,000 years old, many over 3,000 and some over 4,000 as the rings have been counted on one that had died. Baobabs have difficulty in reproducing so there are very few young trees with most of the trees being over 200 years old. The survival strategy they have adopted is that if they get established, usually after several hundred years, they will then live for a very long time. For some reason the trees 'love' this area and have developed this small woodland which is very rare mostly Baobab trees live in isolated small groups.

The owner employed some University experts who calculated the biggest tree, 200 metres away, was probably over 5,000 years old based on X-rays. This tree was huge and even if the estimates are wrong, you can guarantee it is over 4,000 years old.

I confess I got obsessed with this tree and kept giving it a hug. I couldn't leave it alone.

I kept looking at it, thinking;

- If you believed in Jesus, this tree is at least twice as old as when he was born.
- That huge bough growing from the base was probably alive before 1066 and William the Conqueror.
- That huge branch was alive before the English civil war.
- That small to medium branch was alive before WW1.

It is an amazing thought.

The bar was frequented by local Ranchers who would drive miles for a beer and a chat with their mates and would often stay until late, so the bar only closed when the last one went home. During the evening I had many beers and whiskies, until 1am, and would sit on the large root of tree 'drinking in the atmosphere' even though I was getting up at 5am I couldn't go to bed.

Around midnight a local security guard with a large rifle wandered around the campsite and was surprised to see me. We chatted for a while as his English was ok, a nice man. I explained the tree was more than 4,000 years old and twice as old as Jesus (who he had heard of). He was fascinated with the tree, and we talked for a while before he had to wandered off on his patrol. As he went, I could hear him muttering to himself "4,000 years old, 4,000 years old, bloody hell".

It is a big shame that the owner had not talked to the local people about the trees and how old they were. But also, how important they are to the world, as they are rare and precious with a declining population which was already small.

Coastal Redwood trees

On one of my trips, I stopped off in San Francisco to see the Coastal Redwoods and the Giant Sequoia trees. Close to San Francisco is the John Muir National Monument Wood which holds a medium size forest of Coastal Redwoods. Due to difficult access the wood was never harvested so remains an ancient primeval woodland. Coastal Redwoods make excellent building material and as a result 95% of the forests were cut down.

It is hard to describe walking in this wood. It can only be described as walking through the skyscrapers of New York – the tree trunk just keeps going up and up into the sky.

The trees in this wood average between 80 to 100 metres high. The highest record Redwood tree was measured at over 120 metres, this tree is located much further north. The bottom of the tree trunks averaged around seven metres in diameter and c20 metres in circumference – huge. The trees were also close together around 10 metres apart, so it was very gloomy at base level due to the heavy foliage above.

I went in early spring and was amazed how quiet it was – very little noise. I only saw one or two birds all the time I walked in the forest. Just sitting beneath the trees, in the quiet, was an experience hard to describe – I was overawed.

Giant Sequoia trees

These trees live between 1,700 to 2,300 metres up in the subalpine mountain regions of California with heavy precipitation and live in isolated groves rather than in forests.

I had read about several groves located in Yosemite National Park, so I visited for 2 nights at the beginning of April (park opens on the 1st April). As I drove into the park I noticed snow on the ground, thinking this is California and at a latitude that is further south than Spain, of course height is one of the keys to weather conditions.

As I drove higher and higher to the Sequoia trees the snow got deeper and deeper until eventually the road was closed and my destination was 3 miles away. I walked and because I had been whale watching in the Pacific Ocean off Mexico, I didn't have any winter clothes, but luckily, I had boots. I piled on all my T Shirts and raincoat and walked. It was very cold but worth it.

The trees were huge. These are the largest trees by bulk in the world.

They grow to around 70 to 90 metres tall with massive trunks over 12 metres in diameter and over 35 metres in circumference. One tree I saw had a tunnel cut through it allowing a car to drive through it, yet either side of the tunnel the remaining trunk was wider than the tunnel. Cutting a tunnel through a Giant Sequoia tree happened several times in the 1930's as a gimmick, there are several of these trees throughout California.

The wood is brittle so inappropriate for construction so as a result the majority have survived. However, population has always been small, and it is estimated there are only 80,000 trees in the world, all within California. These trees can live up to 2,500 years. Again, just looking at these trees scattered over a wild snowy landscape with no other people around was wonderful.

The walk back was fun, full-on blizzard, and when I got near my car I spotted a hole in the snow, four-foot down was the top of a picnic table. The area near the car where I had walked across was solid compact snow two metres deep.

That evening I dropped just below the snow line in the main Yosemite Valley and camped in one of their tents you could hire for the night. It was so cold even with ALL my clothes on (2 pairs of trousers, 4 T shirts, 2 jumpers etc) that at 2am in the morning I got up and went for a walk underneath a huge rock face and mountain called 'half dome' which was formed by a glacier which cut off one side of the mountain.

There was a full moon and no clouds, so the stars were great – but so bloody cold.

Forest of Cactus

Whilst travelling through the Mexican desert I came across several isolated forests of about a thousand large cacti. The cacti were the second largest in the world called Pachycereus Pringlei and restricted to Northwest Mexico.

They were huge averaging around 15 metres high with some individuals much higher. They have stout trunks up to a metre in diameter and with an average of dozen very large branches but much fewer branches than similar size trees. It is reported that they can weigh around 25 tones and live up to 250 years.

This part of Mexico is barren desert with minimal rainfall, and it often doesn't rain for years so the cactus stores moisture in its flesh. This acts as a good source for many birds and small creatures particularly when the skin is broken, for example by woodpeckers which thrive in this environment.

The individual cacti were widely spread out being around 30 metres apart which allows easy access except walking was difficult over the rocky and very uneven surface. Whilst walking through the forest I was amazed at the abundance of wildlife particularly birds which were directly supported by the cacti, outside these areas the wildlife was significantly reduced.

It was a surreal experience walking through a woody landscape populated by huge cacti the size of trees.

24

Last man out of Petra

Background

We had a family holiday to Jordan when the children were teenagers which covered the Christmas and New Year period, having Christmas in a Muslim country was interesting as nothing was celebrated or mentioned. We toured the length of Jordan visiting an old Roman city, Mount Nero, Wadi Rum and the Dead Sea. However, the highlight was Petra. The first day in Petra the weather was perfect, sunny and warm with blue skies and we had a great day exploring.

Petra was built between 500 and 100 BC and was the centre of the Nabatean kingdom. It is famous for hundreds of Tombs and Temples carved from red sandstone and looks stunning. The old city, where the people lived in tents, was in a basin surrounded by cliffs and large hills onto which the Tombs were carved.

The Hotel was two miles from Petra, and you walked downhill on a track before reaching the Siq. This is the name for the narrow gorge which is a fault in the rock providing an entrance to the city. The Siq is very atmospheric being only six metres wide with vertical rock faces, both sides, 200 metres high, with a flat stone floor. It is quite dark and eerie.

It is a very dramatic entrance.

At the end, coming into Petra, there is an equally dramatic view – The Treasury. A very large tomb carved into the red sandstone cliff. The Treasury is famous for being featured in the "Raiders of the Lost Ark' film. The Treasury is located in a gorge with many equally impressive Tombs and Temples. To the right it opens up to a large basin surround by cliffs and hundreds of monuments.

The other remarkable temple is the Monastery located on a large hill at the far end of the city. It is carved out of rock and is 50 metres high and 60 metres feet wide. It looks stunning and views of the surrounding desert were equally dramatic. We explored all day having lunch in the Roman Amphitheatre where Gladiators fought. The Romans occupied the area for a few hundred years around 100 AD.

Nabateans lived in the desert and were experts at conserving and managing water. When they died out and the Romans left, the site was abandoned due to the lack of water and was only re-discovered in the early 1800's.

Planned dawn visit

I decided that next day I would go into Petra at dawn to soak up the atmosphere and was the only person who was foolish enough to want to do this. I put my alarm on for an early call having checked I could get access at that time.

My alarm went off just before dawn and I looked out of the window. I couldn't believe my eyes – there was thick snow – l guessed it was about 250mm deep. I know it can snow in the Middle East due to the high altitude but given the weather the day before I didn't expect this. So, back to bed as there was no point going into Petra this early as the red sandstone would look poor, and I am not sure I could get access given the conditions. Over breakfast it transpires it was the worst snowstorm for 40 years and the main highway was blocked with tourists and locals sleeping in their vehicles, a few turned up at the hotel in the afternoon looking very miserable.

Due to the weather the groups' plans were cancelled so I asked if Petra was still open.

"Yes, still open" our guide replied. "Right, I am going in, anyone coming", negative response.

At around 10am I walked down the track covered in 200mm of snow, in a light snowstorm, towards Petra. When I arrived at the entrance to the Siq it was beginning to be covered in melt water to about 50mm.

Arriving in Petra it was empty with a small number of local park rangers and the occasional visitor. The atmosphere was wonderful you could see all the Tombs and Temple covered in snow. After a couple of hours wandering around, I came across a Bedouin tent off the beaten track and up one of the surrounding hills.

A young lady tried to sell me something. "Sorry I have no money on me" I replied.

"Ok, would you like a cup of tea?"

"Yes please, but I have no money"

"That is ok, come and sit inside by the fire to warm you up" she waved me in.

We had a nice chat, over tea and several pieces of cake, looking out over Petra whilst being warmed by the fire. She told me that this was the family home for many generations, and she had gone to university but had decided to come home for a while. The other people in the tent were much older but couldn't speak English so I bowed and smiled a few times.

She told me that Petra is now closed and that the Park Rangers were giving people lifts in 4x4wheel vehicles over the tops, however the track through the Siq will still be open.

On leaving I left her a few pounds, in local money, she smiled and said, "You said you had no money!!" "I lied" I replied with a grin, she laughed and bid me farewell.

Walking toward the Siq a Park Ranger with a large 4x4 stopped me and said "You are the last person in Petra, and this is the last vehicle, get in and I will drive you out"

"No, I am from Yorkshire, I walk in and walk out" I replied with a grin

He shook his head and replied "Are you sure, the Siq is full of melt water and be freezing"

"NO, I am fine"

The Siq was knee high in frozen melt water but quite safe, so I ploughed through, cold but determined to walk out. The walk back to the Hotel was a long drag with my trousers wet and cold but I made it.

Last man out of Petra.

25

Stupidest thing I have ever done

I am NOT proud of this and it's totally out of character. However, it happened, and it makes an interesting tale.

Background

It was my first trip to Africa at the age of 30 and we happened to be staying in a hotel on the edge of the Ngorongoro crater, within the Serengeti National Park Tanzania, on New Year's Eve. Ngorongoro crater is a huge collapsed volcano leaving a crater approximately six miles across with steep sides averaging around 700 metres.

The collapsed volcano forms an isolated mountain on a surrounding flat plain which generates its own weather (basically it can rain throughout the year). As a result, the habitat is varied from tropical rainforest on the crater sides to fertile grasslands, marshy areas and freshwater lagoons in the bottom. This range of the habitat and regular rains supports huge numbers and diversity of wildlife.

The hotel on the ridge overlooking the crater was small with several sleeping huts and a central eating and bar area. The best bit were tables and chairs outside so you could hear the wildlife in the evening whilst having a beer. It was also surround by tropical rainforest and from the hotel I saw Elephants and Buffalo less than 70 metres away as well as numerous birds. It was a wonderful spot.

There were 10 of us in the group and we decided that, on New Year's Eve, we wouldn't stay up to midnight as we had been getting up at 5.30am every morning, so have a few drinks and bed at the usual time, around 10pm. Except at 10pm one of the ladies said "Come on we can't go to bed its 'New Year's Eve' and I will go and get my bottle of brandy which is in my room"

"Ok, and I will go for my whisky" I replied.

Sitting outside was wonderful listening to the Lions roaring in the crater and Hyaena's laughing, only 100 metres away, whilst chatting away – a nice atmosphere. Unfortunately, I kept helping myself to the whisky and not realising how much I had drunk. It was only when they started singing 'Auld Lang Syne' in the bar and I stood up and wobbled that I realised that I had a bit too much, easily done.

I joined in the singing and took my glass of whisky with me. After singing 'Auld Lang Syne' I spotted one of the waiter's clearing away my whisky glass with some still in it! So, I grabbed him by the throat, pinned him to the wall and, for some reason, I was about to hit him – why – I have no idea.

Unfortunately, ALL the waiters in the hotel are Masai warriors (nearest town is 100 miles away) and the only people living in the area are the Masai. Some of these warriors worked part time in the hotel as well leading their traditional way of life.

Luckily, I was grabbed and quickly bundled off to bed. I got up at 5.30am next day with a huge hangover and went out on the safari......nothing was said apart from lots of apologies from me.

Several days later I talked to the English Guide who I had built up an excellent relationship and I asked him "Please tell me the truth, what happened?"

"Ok, as you can imagine the Masai were not happy, you don't threaten a Masai without massive offense and they wanted revenge. Luckily the experienced driver, who is half Masai, managed to talk to chief and calm him down and everything was going smoothly with an offer to pay the Masai off.

When suddenly things turned very nasty, and it looked like the Masai were going to come and get you. We had a backup plan that the other driver was going to get you in the back of his vehicle under blankets and drive away in the dark without lights and we started to put this plan into action.

Again, luckily the experienced driver calmed everything down indicating how good your fieldcraft was and that you were not just a stupid tourist. In the end we agreed a 'price in cattle' at 2am" he explained.

"Ok, how much do I owe you, I will pay" I replied

"No, company is paying I have agreed with Head Office in the UK, it has gone down as a first"

"Ok, could you give an indication of how much?"

"No, best to just leave it and I will be 'dining out' of this one when I get home" he replied with a grin.

I did leave all concerned a large tip and a lesson learned.

26

Great White shark looking at me

Background

I visited South Africa prior to my overland trip to Uganda.

My main ambition was to go cage diving with Great White Sharks and South Africa is a hotspot for these sharks as there are huge colonies of fur seals providing lots of opportunities for lunch and dinner.

Great white sharks – now this was very SPECIAL

Can you imagine standing in a cage with gaps between the metal bars about a 1/3 metre square so you could easily put your arm or leg through it AND a four metre Great White Shark swimming slowly past you – so close you could touch it – less than half a metre away.

This shark swam so slowly along the cage and almost paused opposite me with a huge black eye looking directly at me. You could imagine him thinking "What are you? Can I eat you?"

I went on two boat trips. I wanted to go twice so that I could fully appreciate the experience. All together we had 22 Great White Sharks over 2 days – the smallest around 2.8 metres and the biggest 6 metres. The skipper estimated it would weigh over a 3,000lbs and was the largest shark seen that season. At one point she, big sharks are always she, grabbed the decoy seal and pulled the boat against the strong tide, the boat was 30 metres long with 3 decks – a strong girl. And she was heavily pregnant.

The boat held 20 passengers and at any one point 8 divers would go in the cage – usually this would last for between 30 and 45 minutes due to the cold, it was mid-winter, I had 4 dives over the 2 trips. I always took the spot at the end as the sharks always came in to look at the cage and then swim across it and then around the end, at this point the sharks were very close to the cage. I had several sharks coming up to investigate me, eying me up to try and understand what is going on.

Each person would have a FULL wet suit on including shoes and head gear but no breathing apparatus – either air tanks or snorkel as bubbles in the water scared the sharks off as 'unnatural'.

To attract the sharks the boat people constantly put out 'chum – blood and guts' and use both a decoy seal and a large tuna fish on a rope as bait. As soon as a shark approached the bait, they would quickly pull it in to encourage the shark to get close to the cage and boat, on several occasions the shark managed to grab the tuna fish or the decoy.

The fun bit was when a shark attacking the Tuna bait overshot and ended up attacking the cage with its FULL mouth opened – smashing into the cage at face level. This happened to a poor girl who very quickly got out of the cage, screaming and in floods of tears, and quickly had to have a shower and changed her clothes due to an unfortunate incident!!

If it was not your turn to be in the water, you still had excellent views of the sharks from the deck – I took many great pictures. I could also watch the African guys throwing in the 'chum'. Often sharks would come to investigate and, on several occasions came 2 metres out of the water to try and take the guy. He had to be alert and move further up the boat ramp (The boat was open at the back to allow the chum to be discharged into the sea).

I said to the skipper all your crew are white except the black African who throws out the chum, why? He replied straight faced "The black guys are 2 a penny so if a shark gets one there are plenty more" – I guess he was having fun but given my impression of South Africans, over the several weeks I had visited, maybe he was serious!!

Overall, it was excellent – one of the best things I did on my trip through Africa.

Interestingly the cage diving industry in this part of South Africa has now finished because the Great Whites have moved away. Why?

A pack of Orcas (Killer Whales) have moved into the area. There is only one animal, apart from man, that can kill a Great White Shark and that is an Orca. They hunt the shark by flipping it on its back and holding it there until it drowns which only takes a few minutes. The Orca will then eat the shark liver and leave the rest.

27

Mongolia a self-induced ecological disaster area

To some Mongolia is a beautiful country with wide open spaces, few people and big blue skies. However, I thought it was an ecological disaster area.

Mongolia has one of lowest population densities in the world, 2 people per square km. It is huge with the Gobi rocky desert taking up to 50% of Mongolia on its western boundaries whilst in the east the land is fertile supporting large areas of grassland with some tree cover. The train to China went through the Gobi which I loved especially seeing wild camels, but most people thought it was flat, stony and boring.

The main industry is nomadic livestock herding which supports c50% of the population however, in the last 20 years oil and gas has been found which has mostly benefited the elite with some tricklingly down effect.

The country is split into two;

- Nomadic livestock farmers c50% of the population.
- Massive migration of the poor to the capital – Ulaanbaatar. Out of a population of 3.07 million nearly 50% (1.45m) live in the capital.

Migration to the capital is driven by;

- Rural poverty of the 'have not's' due to many failed rainy seasons and especially from over grazing reducing the viability of their small herds.
- Bright young people who want to improve themselves.

Overgrazing on a massive scale

In the last 20 years the wealthier nomadic farmers with access to more land have massively increased their herds due to improved livestock prices especially with exports to China and the impact and circulation of oil money. Nomadic farmers have a variety of livestock including Sheep, Goat, Yaks, Horses (bred for both eating and riding). Livestock volumes have increased from 33million in 2000 to 68 million in 2019. It is clear the land can't support this volume.

The grass is generally 25 to 50mm high with many bare patches which stretch over miles and miles – from valley to the hill tops – there is no respite from hungry mouths. Some of the nomadic farmers drive motor bikes and 4x4 vehicles, though the majority are still on horseback, to herd their livestock. Unfortunately, the land is scarred by vehicle tracks which due to the dry barren earth it erodes and leaves permanent marks.

As the wealthier nomads massively increase their herds the smaller poorer herders can't maintain a healthy profitable business on land where the fertility has been massively reduced. As a result, these people are forced off the land and emigrate to the city.

You can see the evidence of this over grazing by visiting Khustai National Park which sits within the landscape described above. I believe this represents what Mongolia looked and felt like before over grazing. As we approach the park on a rough track the land was grazed by livestock with grass being very short. On entering the park..... what a difference .... the grass was 250mm to 500mm high ....AND the land was full of rodents.... mice and voles. Nomadic farmers and livestock are banned from the park.

Every five metres as we were driving along, I would see rodents running across or alongside the track. The habitat was perfect for rodents ......and, of course, birds of prey love to eat rodents. They were everywhere ...hundreds of hawks, buzzards, eagles and vultures whereas outside the park I only saw 2 birds of prey in 10 days.

Rich grass lands supported large animals in sustainable volumes such as Red and Roe deer and as a result attracts predators such as wolves. The landscape was green, fertile and full of wildlife.

Przewalski horse

This national park is famous as home to the last breed of wild horses.

All species of horses have been manipulated by man.... inbreeding and messing with their genes. The American mustang and Australian brumby are feral horses that have been introduced and manipulated by man. Przewalski horse is the last of the true wild horses.

In the past the horse was widely hunted and due to this pressure the last true Przewalski horse was seen in the wild in 1969. However, a small 'pure' population survived in just two Zoos. In 1992 a small population were released in this national park and have established a breeding population. We managed to spot several groups albeit relatively far away, but you could get a reasonable view.

Genghis Khan....

Born 1162 and died 1227 of natural causes. He ruled the world.

This was all achieved in a relatively short period.... around 20 years. After his death his sons and grandsons etc maintained their overseas territories until 1294 when the empire fractured into separate groups resulting in-fighting at the centre to decide who would be the next leader.

He ruled from Mongolia to Southeast Asia as far as Cambodia to Northern India and as far west as Eastern Europe and the Middle East.

How was he so successful?

- When he started out, he managed to unite the various nomadic tribes in Mongolia under his leadership.
- He trained the men to a high degree with composite bows that are easy to use on horseback.
- Mongolian men 'live on horseback' from a young age so are natural cavalrymen.
- However, the horses are wild and then captured and trained for warfare. But in between fighting they are released back into the wild which makes them strong and tough. Wild horses will fight each other especially stallions who sometimes fight to death but also when conditions are poor such as droughts only tough horses will survive. If the horses are kept and fed all year around, they are generally weaker.
- He split his soldiers into units with separate leaders providing clear lines of command and discipline.
- Crucially he let ALL the soldiers share the plunder usually only the rich keep the 'goods' so the foot soldiers are not as keen to fight and possibly die, but if you think you can set your family up for life then you are more likely to fight and fight hard. Even if you are killed, he still gave land and livestock to the dead soldier's family, his surviving soldiers would witness that he followed through with this promise.
- And, of course, he has a reputation as a great leader whom people wanted to follow.

When he defeated and occupied an area or country, he installed a stable administrative government run by his own people especially his family and later his sons.

And, of course, he killed every man and boy in the occupied area .... he had this rule if you were taller than the 'centre of the axial on a cart' which is about one metre high........ you died.

By killing ALL the men and young boys there was little resistance to the ongoing rule so that he 'left few men' to govern and move on to the next target.

Genghis Khan Statue

The richest person, in Mongolia, who owns most of the oil and gas reserves, decided to build a statue to Genghis Khan.

The statue is massive.... amazing .... brilliant ....and definitely worth seeing. It has a lift inside to take you to the top ...it is 40 metres high.

It is made of stainless steel and is just beautiful........ Genghis khan on horseback.

To build the statue he employed foreign expertise, highly skilled workmen and the best materials. However, the surrounding area including footpaths and outside stairs were built using local workers. When I visited the statue was only 9 years old.

It was magnificent however the surrounding area was falling apart not just parts but the majority. For example, you had a stone stairway that was split and closed for safety reasons whilst the supporting walls were falling down. Mongolians have little tradition of building as they live in tents and being nomadic, they keep moving. This explains why they have poor understanding of construction and its basic science especially where you have permafrost.

To me it was a mess and a disaster zone ....and quite comical.

They had spent millions on a fantastic statue, but the surrounding infrastructure was awful falling apart in less than 9 years. I loved it.

28

Flawed decision making but with the best intentions

In January 1991 I went on an overland trip from England to Poland looking for wolves. It was a good trip, very cold, but interesting especially seeing communist Poland. The Berlin wall had come down 14 months before and Russian troops were in the process of leaving both East Germany and Poland whilst handing power over to the local people. Sadly, there were no wolves.

Our base camp was on the Polish/Russian boarder in a remote hunting lodge in a huge pine forest. The journey across Northern Europe by 4x4 minibus (2 full days driving) was fascinating almost going back in time.

- West Germany ultra-modern.
- East Germany – 1950's. Old vehicles and basic equipment
- West Poland – 1930s.
- East Poland – 1910. Majority of the vehicles were horse drawn carts, all houses had wells for water, and most didn't have power and those that did were by a private generator.

After our wildlife adventure, on the way home, we had an overnight stop in a small East German market town. We had a few hours of day light left so I went for a wander but there was not a lot to see so I just people watched.

I noticed a couple of Vietnamese men and a young lady of European descent. After the Vietnam war many people were re-located to Eastern Europe to help their communist friends during the Vietnam famine, so it is not unusual to see them. They looked very 'shifty' so having nothing else to do I watched them from a distance. They were hanging around outside a large Post Office/Govt building and after c10 minutes they suddenly looked alert and moved off in different directions.

An old lady in worn clothes and looking like she had a 'hard life' came out of the building and walked slowly down the street. The young lady (from above) moved closely behind, pausing and then quickly lifted out her purse, immediately one of the Vietnamese men walked up to her and the purse was exchanged.

She quickly disappeared and the purse minutes later was passed to the other Vietnamese man, who was clearly the boss, he opened the purse, took the out the money, and then posted the purse into a letter box. All done very quickly and professionally.

They all disappeared in different directions for 10 minutes and then met up again – they were jubilant, bouncing around, grinning and looking very smug.

I was furious, livid, 'you robbing bastards'. That poor old lady. It is possible she had just collected her weekly pension, in those days, she probably had little else.

I was livid ......but what could I do.

Tell the police .... but then what? I could be stuck in this small East German town for days if they decided they want to proceed, and I would be the only witness. I could not risk that.

At this point the Boss spotted me watching and stared at me. So, I came up with a 'flawed plan'. I pulled up my collar, put my chin down and mutter something into my collar as though I had a hidden police radio.

It had a great effect. They went into 'panic mod' and ran off.

I was feeling pleased with myself, a very small victory. I then started to go back to the hotel. Unfortunately, after 10 minutes, the Boss appeared on the opposite side of the road and gave me this evil threatening look. The look was vicious and nasty ....it sent a chill right through me. AND he started to cross the road towards me, I quickly dived into a local shop and luckily, he re-traced his steps and kept watch.

What the hell do I do now. I was scared and felt trapped, I didn't want to argue or get close with that man.

Luckily 40 metres away I spotted three people from our group. When they got level, I jumped out and made a big fuss of seeing them again. I quickly explained I was very worried about that Vietnamese man over there and that I will explain, in full, when we get back to the hotel. BUT first we need to get back to the hotel quickly.

"I need to walk two metres in front of you three so that he cannot run in and stab me in the back". I was genuinely worried that might happen, he certainly looked capable.

"You three need to follow me and keep an eye on him". Everything went to plan, and we got back safely.

I explained the tale over dinner and why I was so nervous. We all felt sorry for the poor old lady.

29

Have you ever seen a black lady turn white?

Background

Before I set off on my overland African trip, I stayed at my brother-in-law brother's holiday home in Pringle Bay which is c80 miles east of Cape Town. I stayed for 10 days travelling around watching wildlife. I decided to have a day trip to a National Park which was 200 miles away and set off at 4.30am so that I could miss the traffic but more importantly get there just after dawn.

The reserve has no large predators, so you are allowed to walk the various trails which I did for a few hours and then drove around the reserve looking for more wildlife. The reserve is famous for Bontebox antelope, which is a beautiful creature but due too loss of habitat and hunting the world population is around 500 and this reserve holds an important breeding population. I had several excellent close views of the Bontebox as well as Mountain Zebras which are also rare as well Red Hartebeetse.

Having spent a lovely morning in the reserve I decided to head home around 1pm but first I drove to the visitor's office, in the middle of the reserve, to buy some refreshments for the journey home. Driving slowly up a dirt track 300 metres from the visitor's office I saw something move in the short grass, so I slowed up to have a look and quickly identified it as a large Cobra. I jumped out of the car to have a better look, being a Cobra I kept a distance of about 20 metres and kept my body and face at angle so if it decided to spilt venom I could turn very quickly.

The Cobra lifted his head a couple of inches with a large black eye looking directly at me and then slipped away into the long grass. I carried on to the office to buy my refreshments and mentioned I have seen the Cobra. The office was staffed by two middle aged black ladies in warden uniforms.

"No, No Sir, it would be a tree snake" in a condescending voice.

"Well, I thought it was a Cobra" I replied paying for my refreshments.

"No, No Sir, not a Cobra" in a tone that indicated I was a 'daft English man who been out too much in the sun'.

I jumped in the car and drove 50 metres when I spotted the Cobra coming down the side of the road towards the office, so I stopped and managed to get a picture as it crossed the road. Afterwards I measured the road and based on my picture estimated the snake to be about three metres long, a big snake.

Given the seriousness of the situation I reversed the car and went back into the office.

"Sorry, I think it is Cobra and it is coming this way. And given it is springtime and it is very active at mid-day I suggest it is building a breeding territory so could be aggressive. I have a picture"

"Yes sir, let me see" in an 'I'm still not convinced' tone.

I showed the picture.

"Oh my GOD, bloody hell. Oh my GOD" she cried.

She turned from being black to a pale white, staggered backwards and slumped into her chair shouting "Oh my GOD".

The other lady, who had disappeared, came charging back into the room.

"It's a Cobra, it's a Cobra, it's a Cobra" the first lady cried in a very panicky voice.

"Oh my GOD. Oh my GOD" the other lady cried.

"Right, I will leave it with you…. Ladies" and left with a smug look on my face.

As I drove off, I saw the snake again traveling away from the office about 200 metres away. My guess is the rangers will kill it as trying to catch an aggressive territorial Cobra is very dangerous and obviously can't let it have a territory close to the visitor's office.

30

Falling into Lake Malawi

Background

On my overland trip through Africa, we camped on the bank of Lake Malawi. It is more like an inland sea it is huge, 360 miles long and at its widest 47miles. It is part of the great rift valley running down the eastern side of Africa. It is the ninth largest freshwater lake by water volume and has more species of fish than any other freshwater body. There c700 species of Cichlid, small colourful fish that are often stocked in aquariums. I snorkelled with them, in huge shoals of small brightly coloured fish about 25 to 75mm long.

After travelling by overland truck for 6 hours we quickly threw up our tents (the campsite included a toilet block and bar, so it was one of the better camp sites) and went for much needed refreshing swim. In the lake 50 metres downstream from me were four boys aged around eight. I decided to have some fun and went up and splashed them. After 10 minutes of splashing and laughing I asked for a break so I could talk to them.

One of the boys was clearly bright and could speak perfect English whilst the others struggled. During our conservation he told me that he lived in the local village with his mum and granny and that his dad had died when he was very young, he was a fisherman and one day never came back. It appeared that most children in the village had lost 1 or 2 parents and sometimes live with their Auntie. Average life expectance in Malawi is 34 – due to poverty, Aids or just hard work trying to make a living. Throughout Africa you rarely saw old people and extremely rarely old men.

Fishing in the Lake

I got on extremely well with the guy who ran the overland truck and he arranged for Austin and me to go fishing for 10 dollars.

(Austin was a guy I teamed up with on the trip). We made our way down the beach, in the dark, to several local fisherman at 7pm and climbed aboard their local fishing boat. Except it was not a boat but a huge floating log with no extra ballast strapped to the side. This is the typical boat in the area, just a huge log.

We straddled the log, either end, whilst 2 fishermen perched on top and started to paddle out into the lake. It was very unstable and after paddling 100 metres we both looked at each other down the log and shook our heads. I quickly indicated that we want to go back to the beach and on turning around. I fell in, including my mobile and wallet. I swam back to the beach laughing my head off.

I walked straight back to camp giggling to myself whilst Austin stayed and talked to the fishermen. Local fishmen had mastered the art of sailing these things but you can also understand how many died, in the lake, if a storm arrives.

On reaching the camp I could see the bar area was playing loud music. The top of the bar is unusually wide (three metres) and long (ten metres) made of thick wood and the bar manager loves getting people on the bar to dance. His view is 'more you dance, the more you drink, the more fun you have, the more you drink'.

On arriving at the bar four girls from our truck were dancing away and as soon as they saw me, cried "Mike, come on up".

I thought.... I am wet through, sober but in Africa ...so why not. I got straight up and danced away like a middle-aged bloke, dripping water everywhere.

Who cares .... I am in Africa!!

31

Sitting with a Maned Wolf sniffing the air less than a metre from my face

Background

I went to Brazil on a wildlife trip with the Maned Wolf being one of my targets.

Luckily there is a known spot where monks have been feeding wild Maned Wolves for over 100 years and they have become used to people. It would appear the chance of seeing this usually shy animal were high.

Six Catholic Monks live in a lovely Monastery in a huge private nature reserve. The reserve is hilly with a large area of tropical seasonal rainforest as well as scrub land with many small lakes. The Monastery is made from large stones which form a large square building. At the front is a substantial stairway, 10 metres high and 6 metres wide, leading to a large stone terrace, in front of big wooden doors. It was a lovely place, not stunningly beautiful, basic but full of atmosphere.

The story goes that 100 years ago a young monk noticed that after throwing out the leftover chicken bones, after supper, they soon disappeared. The monk was particularly interested in nature so he stayed up and watched, discovering that a Maned Wolf would appear, almost immediately for a free meal.

Overtime the monk and the Maned wolves developed a relationship where he would put out chicken bones on the large stone terrace, at the top of the stone stairways, and would ring a bell. This was a signal that dinner was ready and quite often a wolf would appear soon afterwards. Maned Wolves are solitary and mainly nocturnal so the monks would ring the bell at 7 pm, it gets dark in the tropics around 6 pm, and the wolves, usually three or four per night, would appear throughout the night, never together usually a couple of hours apart.

The tradition has continued and is famous in wildlife circles for being the best place to see Maned Wolf. Luckily the monks control the numbers to 20 people per night and because it is in the middle of nowhere being several hundred miles from the nearest small town it is well managed.

First, we had dinner in a large basic dining room with solid wooden tables. The food was simple but excellent made by the monks. The group stayed for two nights in the Monastery sleeping in basic rooms, the six monks do everything as there are no other staff. They grow their own food with a huge vegetable and fruit garden at the back of the Monastery.

After dinner, around 7pm, the head monk puts out the chicken legs, at least 50, on a large tray on the stone terrace and then rings the bell. For the next few hours, the 20 visitors, all sat patiently but apart from hundreds of bats flying around we had no wolves.

Time passed and a few of the less keen visitors started to drift off to bed. At mid-night, still no wolves, we were down to eight, of which two were asleep on the terrace.

By 2am it was just me. I decided I am NOT going to bed until I have seen a WOLF even if it is all night. I was sitting at the front of terrace next to the stairway and around 3 am a 'shadow' appeared on the stairs and slowly made its way up.

Maned wolves have very long legs and stand around 1.3 metres high. They are slimmer than grey wolves but are still powerful animals with long fangs.

The wolf appeared at the top of the stone terrace, paused looked around and watched me for a while. It then walked away from me and circled the chicken legs and came and paused less than a metre in front of me. Because I was sitting the down, we looked at each other at face level, he sniffed the air a few times and then wandered off towards the chicken legs to eat.

Considering I have a fear of domestic dogs I felt rather relaxed, knowing that I must not move, or it will frighten him. He stayed for 30 minutes easily eating some of the chicken legs crunching them in his jaws. Luckily one of the guys on my trip had woken up and appeared, just in time, and managed to wake a few others from the trip.

25 minutes after the first wolf left a slightly smaller female appeared.

Talking to the monks in the morning they said it was very unusual for them to come so late and they think there may have been a Puma in the area which had worried them.

I went to bed at 4.30am very happy AND then the alarm went off at 5.30am for a dawn walk. After the walk I had breakfast and then had a long nap. The dawn walk was excellent and found Masked Titi Monkeys which are very rare but with a healthy population in this area.

I also found a Hyacinth Visorbearer, a very colourful hummingbird that is restricted to this side of the mountain in an area of 20 square miles. Strangely there is a very similar bird that lives on the other side of the mountain with a similar restricted range. At some point, in the past, they were the same bird but for some reason the range was split into two and they have developed into different species. Birds and animals can be very similar but if they can't successfully breed, between each other, they are classed as separate species.

32

Threatened by a Bull Elephant

On my first visit to Africa, we visited Tarangire National Park which is a huge reserve of open seasonal tropical woodland, perfect Elephant country.

We slept in tents deep in the bush with no fences, a lovely spot.

I had got into the habit of getting up pre-dawn, 5 am, and having a walk around to soak up the atmosphere and see what wildlife was around. Because everyone is usually still in bed the wildlife is often quite tame, especially the birds. At the various camps I had found some interesting mammals such as Hyenas, Porcupine, Buffalo and various Antelopes, large mammals would often come around the camp at night to avoid the Lions.

This morning, after the sun had risen, I spotted a small herd of Elephants about 600 metres away. I walked to within 100 metres to watch them, at this point I was joined by someone from my group who also liked getting up early.

The lead Elephant was aware of our presence as he looked at us several times but seemed very relaxed as he kept feeding, which was a good sign. We watched them for around 20 minutes as they wandered around feeding. The lead Elephant gradually drifted away from the others and headed towards us but not in a direct line, whilst continuing to feed.

He approached to within 30 metres and then suddenly noticed us, he had clearly forgotten about us. He quickly squared up to us and started to paw the ground whilst lifting his head and opening his ears as wide as he could making him look as big as possible. He was enormous, I remember thinking 'he just filled the sky'.

My companion said we must run.

"NO" I said remembering what my dad I told me (he was a farmer's son) always keep eye contact and never turn your back on an agitated animal.

I told him "Keep facing him and walk slowly backwards, don't turn around"

We walked no more than five or six steps when he lowered his head and started feeding.

We just backed off and went for breakfast.

Best friends

Whilst travelling through Namibia we stopped in Etosha National Park. A huge reserve which is a combination of semi desert with large salt pans but also numerous freshwater springs providing sufficient water to support significant numbers of wildlife.

I was watching a scattered herd of Elephants when I noticed a female Elephant walking, with purpose, towards another female. I noticed the two Elephants when they were 800 metres apart and watched them come closer together. On approaching both Elephants entangled trunks pausing for a few minutes and then moved forward and rubbed their foreheads together.

Sisterly love!

Huffing and puffing Old Male

During my visit to Etosha I went on a night safari in a small jeep. It was a full moon with a clear sky, so the visibility was reasonable.

We had stopped the jeep, turning the engine off, listening to the sounds of the night and absorbing the atmosphere, when out of the gloom a large old bull Elephant appeared and wandered towards us. He knew we were there and was very relaxed as long as we didn't speak or take flash photography. We sat in silence as he made his way towards us and passed by the jeep, about 10 metres away.

The old Elephant was like an old man, huffing and puffing, blowing and passing wind at regular intervals. It was a constant noise. He was a big powerful animal but because he was so relaxed, we never felt in danger. He had very small tusks because there is a lack of minerals, in Etosha, so the tusks are brittle and often break.

The biggest Elephants in the world are in the Okavango Delta. The Elephants are huge and in large numbers. Okavango Delta is the largest inland delta in the world. The water starts in Angolan Mountains over 1,000 miles away, travels via huge rivers and then hits the flat lands of the Okavango. It then spreads out into a huge inland waterway and then disappears into the Kalahari Desert. The scenery of the delta is stunning, a mosaic of channels of water, islands and marshes – plus lots of wildlife.

Indian Elephant

The difference in size between female and male Indian Elephants is remarkable. The females are petite whilst the old males are huge.

The wild population of Indian Elephants, world-wide, has reduced significantly due to land clearance for farmland and poaching. However, in certain places there are healthy populations, for example, Kaziranga National Park in Assam.

I was lucky to see five separate old Bulls, all of which still had their tusks.

These animals are huge with their two-domed forehead and small ears making them distinct. Interestingly all five bulls were single tuskers which is not uncommon in this park and each tusk was between 3 to 5 metres long – biggest tusks I have ever seen.

33

People

I love travelling to meet people from different cultures learning about how they do things, think and live.

When I grew up, I was taught certain things such as 'how to write' starting from top left-hand corner – left to right – and then down the page, of course, using the line as the base line', as well as the 26 letters in our alphabet.

This, plus, everything else I was taught, was 'that is how you do it' so I assumed that everyone, in the world, did it that way as I was not told anything different. The only exception, as a young child, I knew that people spoke different languages.

What I love it that different cultures have the same problems as us but come up with a completely different solution. Like writing, how to eat or religion, there is no right answer.

Travel broadens the mind, if you allow it.

Where you get mass tourism it can corrupt the local culture, 'chasing the tourist dollar' can have a negative effect albeit this is a generalisation and there are huge numbers of genuine people in these areas.

Whistles and Clicks

Talking must be the same everywhere – we just have different languages.

As a child I understood that most of countries have their own language and, of course, even in a small country like England you get regional variations. I realised, early on in my life, words both spoken and written were just a code and if the other person understands the code you can communicate. My assumption, of course, was that everyone uses words.

Later in life I learnt that some small tribes speak with whistles and clicks. I had the pleasure whilst staying in the Kalahari Desert to meet five ladies from the San Bushpeople tribe.

We stayed on a remote farm ranch where we were allowed to camp in the bush next to the farmhouse, it was a rarely visited site that just provided a bit of extra pocket money, the main business being cattle ranching. The farm was owned by the 4th generation of western settlers and the current owner, and her father had, over 30 years, managed to build a relationship, albeit a distant one, with the local San tribe who continue to live a nomadic hunter gather existence. However, given the chance they love to smoke and drink alcohol introduced by us.

The owners asked if a few San people would come and show us their bushcraft, for a payment in food, at say 4pm. However, they don't have watches and 4pm is roughly when the sun goes to a certain point in the sky.

Five ladies wandered in at 5.15pm, two of the young ladies had their 'boobs' hanging out. All very causal.

One of the ladies spotted a 'cigarette butt end' on the floor and was quickly grabbed and put behind the ear for later. They wandered around the bush showing us certain plants, making fire from sticks – all very unprofessional but fun.

The best bit was how they communicated to each other (not us). They used words but also clicks and whistles – about 50% words and rest a combination of clicks and whistles. I could not work out a pattern or period when words dominated – it was a constant mixture moving easily between the various communication methods. The bush women could only speak their language whilst the camp owner could just about communicate with them but not very well, she tried to explain what was going on but most of the time she didn't know.

Helping to protect and understand the Bush people has been her passion for the last 30 years. Her father went from disliking them to appreciating them over this period. Her Grandfather regularly shot them especially on a Sunday as it was his day off, Sunday afternoon sport (told to me in private by the camp owner).

However, even now she can only just communicate them and when I asked "Do you understand them" – "No way, they are still a mystery, but they have survived in this harsh environment for more than 30,000 years" she replied with pride.

Ecuador – in the 'cloud forest'

I was on a wildlife trip with a small group, six in total, in the Andes Mountains in the 'cloud forest' about 2,000 metres above sea level.

We were walking along a rough track bird watching as we went and came across a remote house, which had seen better days, when the children came rushing out to greet us. They were clearly poor, torn and tatty clothes but clean. The children were followed by the mother who had a conversation with our guide about what we were doing. Our guide explained we were looking for birds, at which point the lady indicated that she feeds the birds and has many Hummingbirds and we are welcome to see them. Our guide asked us what we want to do.

I replied "Let's be nice, it is only there, and we don't have to stay long"

The others agreed and soon we were sat down outside her home, watching the Hummingbirds and drinking tea, which she had made us. It was very welcoming.

Kids, of course, thought it was wonderful, staring at us and then running away.

Upon leaving as a thank you I offer her some money for the tea. She totally refused, no, she would not accept. So, I point to the bird feeders, of which there were many, and indicated the money was for the bird food, at this point she accepted.

Hopefully, she would use it for the family – proud hardworking people.

Burma

Again, a small group of four of us were walking alongside a river when we came across a small village. Each house had a courtyard and a surrounding fence to keep the chickens in. One house had the gate open, and I could see an old-fashioned sewing machine on the table in the courtyard. I looked in whilst still being outside.

Our guide, who was wonderful, asked if I was interested and I replied, "My wife loves craft work, and I was interested in the sewing machine". Before I could stop her, she was inside the courtyard talking to the owner who ushered us in.

The daughter of the owner, aged about 20 who could speak some English, made us feel very welcome, making us tea, showing me the sewing machine (which I was not that interested in, but went along with it) as well as chatting about themselves and what we were doing.

They also showed me their home, the kitchen and living room. It was very basic the floor was just trodden earth, tatty bits of broken furniture and bits of plastic boxes.

It transpires the sewing machine was used to manufacture items for a local businessman who sold them in the local markets. I offered to buy a T shirt, but she said it was all made to order so I offered some money as a gift for the baby (the daughters' baby slept throughout the visit) she refused.

Proud hardworking people.

I love kids

Kids everywhere in the world are great, all they want is to have some fun if they are sufficiently fed and watered. If they could speak a bit of English, I would talk to them and tease them. If they could not, I would nod and grin, they would often just stare back at you.

My most memorable incident happened as we were just leaving Namibia, we were in a smalltown getting supplies, and I realised I had c£5 in Namibian currency left over. A short distance away were two young children just about to cross the road. They were clearly very poor and had come from the local school in school uniform but theirs were much worse than others, tatty with many holes and very grubby. The oldest was about eight and looked like the older sister holding hands with a young boy about four years old. She was clearly in charge and looking after him on the way home.

I called out to her and went up to her, giving her the money. She was not comfortable with dealing with strangers or foreigners, so she grabbed the money and pulled the young lad across the road in a hurry.

Stopping once she had crossed the road, she looked at the money, and then just looked back at me, staring 'opened mouthed' speechless. She held this pose for many minutes. As the expression goes 'she was gobsmacked'.

A small gesture from me that made my day and hopefully their day assuming it was not taken from them.

34

I confess, I like to swim in various seas and oceans as well as collecting water to bring home

Background

I love to 'tick off' various seas, oceans and freshwater rivers/lakes that I have swum in across the world, sad but true. I can't resist a quick swim, if I have the opportunity.

I also have a hobby of collecting a 'jar of water' from similar bodies of water, even if I have not swum in them.

It is my main souvenir of the trip.

Lake Baikal – Siberia Russia

It is unique and the statistics are incredible.

- Largest freshwater lake, by volume, in the world.
- Holds 20% of the world's liquid freshwater.
- Considered to be the deepest lake in the world, 5,354 feet (c1,600 metres) deep.
- It was created as a 'rift valley' which is a large fault in the earth and then flood.
- 397 miles long and at its widest 49.
- It is a very isolated lake in the middle of Siberia. There is one small village on the whole lake.
- It has a huge number of endemic plants and animal species, estimated at over 3,000.
- Many large endemic fish such as Baikal Salmon (does not migrate) and Omul a very tasty fish eaten raw, I love it.
- Unique freshwater seal, called Nerpa, which doesn't migrate and survives the winter in pockets of open water. I managed to see 2 so was very happy.

- Oil fish, called Golomyanka. It lives at the bottom of the lake and due to the pressure, it has no swim bladder, just oil. 40% of the body is oil and if you put it in a frying pan it disappears. At night it comes to within 100 metres of the surface, where they capture them. I bought two, the size of my little finger, at a cost of £8. I asked the local guide if I could eat them raw, "yes" he replied with a shudder. It was like eating cooking oil.

Much to the amusement and astonishment of the group and the local leader I asked if I could go for a swim from the boat we had hired for a trip on the lake.

"Ok, but it will be cold, it is late September" he replied

"It will be right"

They landed the boat on a remote beach and in I went.

Cold, yes, but brilliant as well as collecting a 'jar of water' for my collection. My fellow passengers thought I was a 'mad Englishman' and took 'tons' of photographs.

Dead Sea

One of the strangest experiences I have had, is trying to swim in the dead sea. It is exhausting as the heavy water forms a strong barrier and is very difficult to swim 10 metres.

The best bit was standing up right, in the water, with 20% of the top part of your body above the surface. You can stand up right for minutes at a time, however, if you lose your balance, you flip over. If you flip backwards, it kills your back forcing a tight curve and once you start to flip you can't stop it.

I also did the tourist thing and read a newspaper whilst laying in the sea and it is not a gimmick you can read a newspaper whilst bathing.

Again, the statistics are amazing:

- Lake surface is 1,412 feet (430 metres) below sea level and is part of the Jorden Rift Valley which continues through East Africa.
- Salinity level is 34% – 10 times saltier than the oceans.
- It is 31 miles long and 9 miles at its widest point whilst being 978 feet (300 metres) deep at is deepest point.
- The overall lake is shrinking and many hotels which were at the water's edge are now 400 metres away.
- Bathing in the dead sea was very fashionable in the early 1900's as it was thought the minerals, in the sea, were good for the body and general health. The fashion has now changed, and the hotels are 'tired and run down'.

Hot natural springs near Mount Bromo, Indonesia

Sarah and I climbed Mount Bromo to witness sun rise and you can peer into the crater to watch molten lava. Mount Bromo is in East Java Indonesia and stands 2,329 metres high.

It is an active volcano last erupting six years before we visited. The crater is mainly 'cooled lava' but there are large patches where the lava is still in the molten state, being bright red and moving around. We set off at 1 am on horseback for a five-mile ride across a 'cold lava field', from the last eruption, before climbing the cone in the darkness.

We arrived just before dawn to watch the sun come up which is a traditional ritual that local villagers do, on selected dates, to give offering to the gods, this often includes 'live chickens' being thrown into the crater.

A very memorable trip.

In the afternoon we relaxed in a natural hot spring close to Mount Bromo.

The water varied from 30c to 45c at the nearest point to the spring entrance. 45c was 'far too hot' and very uncomfortable whilst water in the 30 to 35c range was very pleasant and the spring water formed a large lagoon allowing you to swim around.

Surrounding the lagoon was verdant tropical vegetation with butterflies and birds flicking around, a beautiful spot. We travelled in 1983 when Java was relatively undiscovered so there were no more than 10 people at the springs, I am sure things will have changed now.

Antarctic Ocean

Believe it or not I have swum in the Antarctic Ocean albeit briefly.

The ship visited this amazing Island, called Deception Island, which is an old volcano rising from the sea floor and many thousands of years ago the cone collapsed leaving a huge crater. On a relatively small section of the crater wall the sea has created a small entrance, approximately 400 metres wide and 800 deep allowing small to medium boat safe access.

Once inside, the crater opens to a large perfect harbour, five miles in all directions. The steep volcanic sides vary between 600 to 1,200 metres high, all of which, rise straight from the water's edge. Penguins have colonised these slopes even to the very top!

In the past the crater, a natural harbour, was used by the whaling fleets and there are stories of the water being covered in Blue Whale carcasses for miles.

The volcano is extinct but hot steam is still produced and one spot on the beach next to the sea hot water flows. So, you can cheat and swim in warm Antarctic waters which I did, but knowing this was cheating three of us walked 100 metres away from the hot stream and dived in, bloody cold.

Straight in and out within seconds.

Collecting 'jars of water' from around the world

A very strange hobby but is fun especially when people see what you are doing and thing you are mad. It started when my equally mad sister, Celia, presented us with a jar of Northumberland water during a severe drought in the rest of the country. This was in the mid 80's.

I took inspiration from this when I started to travel. Of course, my friends think it is fun as apart from the Dead Sea, where you can see the salt at the bottom, all the jars look exactly same and could be tap water.

My collection is currently 28 and range from Mekong River, Persian Gulf, Brahmaputra River, Pantanal, Red Sea, Lake Malawi, Zambezi River, Java Sea, River Nepo the main tributary to the Amazon, Okavango Delta as well as many Seas and Oceans.

Sad but true.

35

Sad things in modern history

I think it is important to go and see, as well as pay your respects, to places where great injustices and sadness has happened in history especially modern history.

You can never understand why these things happen and how cruel man, mostly men, can be to each other. Of course, what drives this is their belief there is a hierarchy of people in the world and that all men are not equal. The scale of this hierarchy means that those at the bottom are thought to be worthless to be exploited or/and killed, the hierarchy is the justification.

Rwandan Genocide

From our base camp in Uganda, on my overland trip, three of us decided to have a full day trip to Rwanda, which was only 30 miles away. We hired a car and driver setting off at 5 am to get to the capital, Kigali, in time for breakfast, at an American Café, with 'real coffee' and full English breakfast, first for three months.

Rwandan Genocide Museum

In 1994 over a three-month period the local Hutu tribe massacred 630,000 Tutsi (80% of the Tutsi population).

The Hutu's tribe forms 85% of the Rwandan population and have always been underprivileged and subservient to the local Tutsi (remaining 15% of the population) elite who own the wealth and property in Rwanda. This separation has been in existence for many years and was made worse by the Belgian colonists who greatly favoured the Tutsi whilst leaving the Hutu's disenfranchised.

There are many different theories of what started the genocide or why it happened.

It did happen and was truly awful.

Most of the killings were undertaken by neighbours or fellow villagers who had known each other for years, often using machetes or other primitive methods.

The museum was excellent and very upsetting. I cried for long periods as it told individual stories and had pictures of the massacre.

Two stories stood out and these are summarised below:

- This young girl, aged eight, survived after being left for dead. Her parents (Tutsi) owned a small farm and employed two Hutus who often played with the children (she had two younger brothers) and would share a family meal with their parents around their dining room. The girl saw them as part of the family. One day both Hutus were very agitated when suddenly they grabbed the younger brothers and then swung them around smashing their heads against a concrete wall, killing them. "Why are you doing this, I thought you were my friend" she cried. "I been told to" they replied. And did the same to her, fortunately she survived the impact.
- A Catholic priest encouraged c2,000 Tutsi to seek shelter and safety inside the church as that would protect them. Once the church was full, they closed and locked the door and then burnt the church down, killing everyone. This happened many times and was clearly planned with full co-operation by catholic priests.

The French peace keeping force did little to help and when Tanzanian troops came in to restore order the French allowed c2m Hutus to escape to the Congo to avoid prosecution, hence why there are ongoing problems in that area.

After that visit we needed a hard drink or two.

So, we went to Hotel Rwanda, a famous businessman's hotel that tried to help people during the genocide. There is also a famous movie about this called 'Hotel Rwanda'.

Killing field of Cambodia

It is estimated that over a million people were killed by the Khmer Rouge between 1975 and 1979. The communist leader behind this was Pol Pot who's focuse was on the middle classes, professionals and intellectuals.

One theory why this happened is that Pol Pot lived in a village near the North Vietnam Ho Chi Minh trail that North Vietnam used to transport supplies, during the war, to the south. There were, in fact, a large series of trails running North to South collectively known as the Ho Chi Minh trail. Most of the trails ran through Laos and Cambodia before entering South Vietnam. The US repeatedly bombed this area as well as using 'agent orange' a chemical to destroy the vegetation. Cambodia because of this bombing is classed as currently the most bombed country in the world, even more than countries in WW2.

It's thought that during this period Pol Pot visited the capital, which was many miles away from the trail, and where life continued as normal with a thriving French café culture and many upmarket restaurants all open and full of wealthy middleclass people without a care in the world, whilst the villages he came from had suffered so much.

We first visited an old school that had been turned into an interrogation and torture centre. It was brutal with various torture equipment on show as well as photographs of the inmates.

Pol Pot had this theory 'It is better that 10 innocent men die than 1 guilty person goes free', rather sobering thought.

We then visited the 'Killing Fields' where they executed thousands of prisoners but first the prisoners had to dig their own grave. Most of the time they killed them by hitting them on the back of their heads with a large Bamboo stick.

There is a commemorative Stupa filled with skulls as a mark of respect.

Very sad.

Nazi Holocaust

Sarah and I visited Auschwitz and Birkenau which was incredibly sad and moving especially seeing the railway line that delivered new prisoners which is often shown in historic photographs.

The Holocaust is well documented.

We stayed in Krakow and visited a nice bar where I overheard 3 ladies (late twenties) talking about what they could do whilst in Krakow, "Why not visit Auschwitz?" one enquired.

"Oh no, why do we want to go there, it will be boring" both replied

Very sad, I was attempted to say something, but Sarah said, NO.

I think everyone has a duty to pay their respects and to reflect on history.

Poland in WW2

During my road trip across Poland, we would come across "war crime sign' which was often next to a bare field. At some point in the WW2 the Germans had destroyed the village and killed all the villagers, all that was left was a bare field.

The most chilling was a huge field with a 'war crime sign'. At this spot in 1941 the Germans surrounded 46,000 Russian Officers with barbed wire and left them to starve to death, they were not provided with food or water. The last man died after 3 months, eating the corpses of the dead.

What is staggering is the German guards just stood and watched this happen.

South Africa Cape Town and apartheid

I wanted to understand more about apartheid, so I visited District 6 Museum.

District 6 was an area in Cape Town just outside the city centre with a population of c100,000 mainly black African and some Asian families. It was documented as a vibrant place with thriving music halls and many lively bars and was often visited by young white people from the nearby white districts. In the 1960's the apartheid Government decided, as the white population was expanding, they were getting too close to district 6, so they decided to move the entire population giving them 90 days to move. The government had built poor quality housing many miles away and had deliberately split up neighbours so 'breaking the community spirit'.

The key point here was that the authorities were nervous that if young white people learnt to live and socialise alongside black people, they would start to ask awkward questions. The authorities would not allow any dilution of their overall message that whites are far superior.

However, the people didn't want to go as it was a community even though it was run down. So, the government sent in the police and troops with lorries to empty the district of people and their possessions at gun point. The photographs of this were on display at the museum including one, which stuck in my mind, of numerous policemen and many large snarling police dogs straining on their leads.

Slave trade

It is estimated that over a million slaves worked the land in South Africa.

I visited a slave trading post whilst I was in Cape Town. It was a very large circular stone building with no windows and, in the past, thousands of people were crammed in before being processed as slaves.

I had not realised that there was an overriding slave strategy. Basically, if you enslaved African people to work in Africa and they escaped they could walk home, even hundreds of miles, which some did at the beginning of the programme. To supply the slaves for South Africa they were sourced from India and the Far East particularly Malaysia. African slaves sourced in South Africa were captured and then sent to the West Indies so that both groups were isolated from home and if they escaped there was nowhere to go.

The South African apartheid system had the whites at the top and then came 'brown or yellow' skin people majority originating from slaves, and then the blacks. So, the native population, in their own country, was 'bottom of the pile'.

I also visited a similar slave trading post in Zanzibar which held people taken from the mainland, again, isolated by 15 miles of ocean. This trading post was run by the Arabs to supply slaves for the middle east and had been operating since the 10th century.

Slavery was a worldwide issue run by the powerful over the weak and, it is believed, still exists today to a very much smaller extent.

36

So close but not to be

Kilimanjaro

As part of my first trip to Africa I attempted to climb Kilimanjaro the highest mountain in Africa at 19,341 feet (5,895 metres). It is a huge volcano and is the largest stand-alone mountain in the world, as the surrounding land is only 600 metres feet above sea level.

There are five vegetation zones as you climb the mountain each with its own ecosystem, these are:

- 600 to 1,500 metres previously Savanna Grassland but due to its fertile soil it is now mostly cultivated by small scale farming.
- 1,500 to 2,700 metres, Montane Rainforest because Kilimanjaro rises so high from the surrounding land it generates its own climate especially rain which occur all year around so supporting tropical rainforest.
- 2,700 to 4,000 metres, Alpine Heath and Moorland.
- 4,000 to 5,200 metres, Alpine Desert and Arctic Tundra
- 5,200 to 5,800 metres, Ice Cap and Frigid zone.

We started walking from 1,500 metres through tropical rainforest with monkeys and birds scattered around but difficult to see. A lovely walk even when it rained as it frequently does in the rainforest. There were 10 of us in the group and one guide who suddenly stopped us. In front, but out of sight, was a small herd of Elephants crashing through the forest, at a guess 70 metres in front.

Our group was support by porters who carried huge loads up and down the mountain as all food, drink and supplies had to be carried up, there is no vehicle access.

First base camp. This was at c3,000 metres and two people had bad mountain sickness especially bad headaches so dropped out and returned to the original camp. First base camp was fairly grotty with the immediate surrounding area used as a dumping ground, but it did a job. The highlight of the evening was seeing a small herd of Elland grazing on the mountain side.

Next day we walked through the Alpine heath and Moorland zone.

The heath is similar to the species that grows in the UK but grows to 15 metres high. It feels very odd walking through a woodland of heath. Luckily the grouse are the same size as our grouse.

Later in the afternoon we went above the vegetation line into open Alpine desert country. We had great views of Kilimanjaro with the peak and ice cap. As it is a stand-alone volcano there is nothing to see from the mountain, the plains below were covered in mist.

Second base camp was at c4,000 metres and was wonderful. A lovely camp, nice views and the surrounding environment was in pristine condition.

Best bit were the hundreds of Striped Grass Mice who were fearless. They would walk up and down the dinner table whilst you were eating and help themselves from your plate!!!

They were everywhere and had no fear of man. We slept on the floor, in wooden huts and needed to close the door immediately or the mice would walk in. We also needed to check our sleeping bags before going to bed, as they often crawl inside for a sleep.

Next day we walked to the last base camp – c4,800 metres.

We walked across a large open plain covered in volcanic ash and because of the extreme altitude only few small plants grew. As a result, there were few birds, but we had a great view of a Lammergeyer Vulture.

This was a long day gradually gaining height, but progress was slow because of the high altitude and the lack of oxygen. At this altitude there is 50% less air than at sea level, the oxygen in the air is the same proportion, therefore there is 50% less oxygen. The lack of oxygen makes walking harder and you often have to stop to take a 'double breath'.

For most of us this is where Mountain Sickness started to kick in with bad headaches and feeling poorly. I felt great – no headache – felt physically fit and heathy.

Third base camp was basic.

We were all tired due to the lack of oxygen, so we ate and went to bed early.

I had a great night sleep with fleas – I was bitten all down my back.

We set off at **1am for the summit.**

Why 1am?

At the upper reaches of the mountain there is a huge steep scree slope that at night is frozen together and therefore much easier to climb. Also, you want to be on the top of Africa to see dawn and the sun come up over the continent.

We climbed, in the dark, up the steep cone for many hours making slow but steady progress. At that height there are no clouds or light pollution, so you had a wonderful view of stars and the moon. There was just sufficient light from the moon and stars to climb without using our torches which provided a wonderful atmosphere.

Eventually we had reached the Frigid zone – cold zone without vegetation.

We climbed steadily to around 5,300 metres – at this point there were only two of us left out of a starting group of ten – my companion was 70 years old but a lifelong walker who was very fit.

We had reached the ice level and started to climb the ice and scree. You could see the glacier around us. I was feeling fantastic, strong and fit and no sign of altitude sickness – no headaches, nothing.

BUT suddenly I vomited and vomited.

I stopped and rested, set off again – vomited – I dropped down 5 metres and rested for 20 minutes – then set off again – on reaching the same point I vomited but with nothing inside me, painful. Then I vomited blood and felt rubbish.

I knew I could not go on – I physically could not move forward without vomiting.

There appeared to be an invisible line that I could not cross as soon as I tried to go beyond it – I vomited.

As soon as I dropped 15 metres, I felt better so I turned around and started to climb but as soon as I got to the same hight as before I vomited again and again.

No good I had to accept defeat.

As soon as I had dropped 15 metres I felt better and then at 150 metres felt great.

Talking to the Porters and professional guides they thought I may have started to get 'High Altitude Cerebral Edema' or 'fluid on the brain'. I had many 'funny turns' for 3 days afterwards each lasting a few minutes – I would feel dizzy, disorientated and unsteady on my feet, which is a common side effect.

Fluid on the brain is a serious case of mountain sickness.

Of course, I was massively disappointed not to reach the summit especially as I felt so good before the mountain sickness kicked in.

Again, talking to the professional guides they estimate only 1 in 10 manage to achieve the top which from my experience, in the few days, on the mountain appear to be a fair estimate. I believe now with modern drugs the proportion reaching the top has significantly increased.

So close but not to be.

However, my nephew Alistair Hall, on a different trip, managed to climb to the top and saw dawn over Africa – well done Alistair.

37

Best bar in the world

Background

In 2007 I travelled to Brazil, particularly the Pantanal, the world's largest wetland, bigger even than England. I visited in the dry season where the wildlife is crowded around the remaining water in small lakes and waterholes.

Local people travel around the Pantanal by either boat or on horseback. Cowboys exist in large numbers working on the cattle ranches. The cattle ranchers and wildlife coexist together except there are some issues with the cowboys killing Jaguars that prey on the cattle. Cattle ranching is low density, around one cow per 100 hectares.

To help transport the cattle to market they have built a dirt track 150 miles long which in the wet season is mostly under water. Even though the road is 150 miles long it only goes a third of the way into the Pantanal. This road is great for wildlife viewing as it gives easy access to the surrounding countryside and many roadside water holes. It is also a very quiet road with only two to three lorries per day.

There are only three locations along the road to stay, the final one was at the end of the road which finishes by a huge river. The first two were specialist wildlife lodges with accommodation for c20 people whilst the final one was a specialist fishing lodge. We stayed at all three places.

Best bar in the world

After travelling around the Pantanal by boat and 4wheel drive, for a week, we stopped on the road at one of the small wildlife lodges.

I spotted, a mile from the lodge, an isolated bar by the side of the road.

Early morning, we had been out watching wildlife and after lunch we had some free time, during the heat of the day, before going out in the evening and night 'spot lighting' for nocturnal animals and bats. I announced over lunch that I was going to the bar and was anyone interested. A couple decided to join me, the rest went to bed for an afternoon sleep.

So, we wandered off to the bar. The bar was basic – 3 wooden tables and chairs, all situated outside, attached to a small house. This was the first house we had seen for 50 miles. All it sold was local cold lager which was very drinkable especially in the heat. We chatted to the bar lady who lived in the house and the bar provided small additional income whilst her husband was a cowboy working on the cattle ranches.

Her main customers were lorry drivers and commercial fishermen, who fish the large rivers. She had on average between three and five customers per day. As it was attached to the house, she could do her chores whilst earning a bit of extra cash.

I loved the isolation – a rough and ready bar surrounded by countryside including a waterhole next to the road. From the bar we could see 2.3 metres tall Jabiru storks, Caiman and Capybaras as well as many birds.

Drinking beer watching wildlife in the most isolated and unexpected bar – excellent.

We sat around a large table with me being furthest from the bar and next to a large 'horse drinking trough'. After a few beers I spotted a very large Bull wandering slowly down the dirt road towards us. To start with, I ignored it, but as it wandered in my direction and got closer, I became slightly more nervous.

My anxiety levels grew as it headed straight towards me and was only 20 metres away. The bar lady laughed at me when she saw my anxiety growing "He is an old softy and coming for his afternoon drink".

At this point the bull with large horns was three metres away and I stood up, much to the amusement of the bar lady and my two friends, who were sitting the opposite side of a large table. Standing up I still had to look up to this great animal, it must have been 2.5 metres high at the shoulder.

Bar lady said laughing "Sit down he is only coming in for a drink, they maybe one of the largest breeds of cattle but are mild mannered and the old bull is a big softy".

So, I sat down with my thigh less than a metre from this huge bull's head and horns. I was not happy but tried to calmly drink my beer whilst keeping a close eye on him.

After a long drink both the bull and I, with my two friends, went our separate ways.

Most enjoyable beer

Interestingly this was on the same trip as above.

We stopped for five nights at the fishing lodge at the end of the 150-mile dirt track. This was a famous sports fishing area for rich Americans to catch Giant Catfish that grew to over 1,000lbs. The American sport fishermen would fly down in light airplanes and fish for a few days, the airfield was just a grass field. The lodge could sleep c20 people in small huts with a communal dining area. This was the low season for fishing, so we had the place to ourselves.

The area in the last few years had become a great place to spot Jaguars that liked to rest up on the riverbank during the day. Jaguars love water and often hunt in the water for caiman. Early morning and late afternoon we would go out on a boat searching for Jaguars – we found three.

In the evening we would 'spotlight' from an open top old army truck for nocturnal animals often arriving back between 11pm and midnight. Even though we were getting up at 6am I couldn't go straight to bed. The lodge had a bench on the riverbank, and I would sit there with a beer every night.

What made it special was that the weather was 'still and calm' and the stars were out in all their glory. Add to that was the sound of male Jaguars roaring every five minutes over their territorial claims.

I could hear three male Jaguars – two directly opposite me on the other bank but slightly apart and then one behind the lodge which was a fair distance away. The two opposite me made huge amount of noise obviously their territories slightly overlap to both their annoyance.

What a way to enjoy a beer – listening to Jaguars disputing their territories.

About 800 metres further down the river was a small heavily fenced compound, with lights, with a dozen horses for the cowboys to herd the cattle. Most nights they were peaceful either grazing or sleeping. But on one night they 'kicked off' big style.

Jumping up and down, kicking the fence with a huge thud and making massively amount of noise. They were not happy and very scared to the point you could hear them shaking with fear. It was very likely that either a Jaguar or Puma was wandering around, and they could smell it.

Strangest thing I have seen in a bar

Whilst travelling in Australia I visited a small remote outback town called Oodnadatta that was over 500 miles north of Adelaide. It had a population of c200 who were mainly Aboriginals.

I decided to visit the Bar which only served local white ranchers, Aboriginals were barred (it was 1983).

The bar is known for having a bar lady who had worked there all her life and was tattooed ALL over her body, of which, she was very proud and saw them as a 'works of art'. In her 'will' she left money to have herself skinned, framed and then displayed, in a very large glass picture frame, on the bar wall for future generations. The skin was quite dark and wrinkly, but you could make out certain tattoos – very odd.

It had several faded newspaper cuttings, also framed, that told the story. When did she die and had her skin framed? – I can't remember the date.

Great view – Stone Town Zanzibar

A lovely little town with huge amount of history – it was the main base for the Arab slave trade from 8/9th century. The Arab slave trade was huge and lasted until the late 1800s.

Stone Town was generally a laid-back community but a few of the locals would hassle you for a quick buck, but I liked the place.

The best bit was meeting for 'sunset drinks' in an old fashion hotel on a large stone terrace overlooking the Indian Ocean with the sun going down straight in front of us. It was drinks, all round and lots of photographs of the sunset with the traditional dhow sailing boats being silhouetted against the evening sunset which lit up the sky in various shades of red.

It was so good we went every night for three evenings.

Stone town is also the birthplace of the Queen lead singer – Freddie Mercury – I found the flat where he was born, very much a 1930's council type flat that was nothing special but that wasn't the point.

It is true Russians can drink

I travelled on the Trans-Siberian railway from St Petersburg to Hong Kong breaking the journey at various points of interest like Moscow.

Altogether a journey of 7,000 miles in six weeks with the longest continuous train journey being three days and nights.

During the stretch through Central Siberia two of us wandered down to the buffet carriage for breakfast – food varied from 'inedible to excellent' – trouble was you didn't know what you were going to get!

Whilst having breakfast two professional looking Russians, estimated to be late 30s, sat opposite us and order a bottle of Vodka and chatted between themselves.

Then they ordered another.

They tried to talk to us but as neither could speak each other's language, so we didn't get very far. We sat and chatted between ourselves and watched the forest go by.

They then ordered a third bottle of Vodka much to our amazement.

We wandered back to our carriage, and I had the habit of standing in the corridor to watch the scenery go by. After 30 or so minutes the 2 Russians staggered passed us – the last one stopped and stared at me whilst looking totally confused and wobbling back and forth – then after a few minutes grinned and wandered off to bed. Totally drunk.

Drinking Competition

We stayed in the centre of Xian whilst traveling through China on my railway journey from St Petersburg to Hong Kong. We were recommended a local restaurant close to the hotel so as a group we went. It was a large place but with many rooms and for the 10 of us we had our own room with a large round table that goes around so that you can 'help yourself' to the various dishes.

The atmosphere, staff and food were all excellent.

In the next room was a party for c40 people of all ages but many in their late 20's to early 40's, and clearly been drinking for a few hours. There appeared to be more males than females and all the young males sat together. Before our food arrived a couple of guests from next door came into our room to stare and wave as us. At this point our food arrived and they left us to our food, very polite.

So, after food, I announced to my group I am going next door....to the look of shock......no worries, I was off.

The welcome next door was excellent .... all the young men jumped up.... smiles and hand waving, more beer was ordered. I stood there with a beer in my hand, grinning and hand waving, obviously, I couldn't speak their local language and they could not speak English, grinning and smiling, enjoying the moment.

I worked out that it was an old man's birthday.... maybe mid 70's.... so I made an effort by showing my respect by walking to his table, giving a short bow with my hands together.

He loved it ...... they loved it.

At this point a young man challenged me to a drinking competition. Of course, I won.... much to the delight of his friends and relatives of the loser..... a westerner beating a local man.

More beer and shots and then hugging and grinning.

Judging it was time to go, I went back to my room and then more beers arrived, paid for by the group next door.

All to help the English Chinese relationships.

38

I hate things near my face
especially near my eyes

Thousands of Bats

When visiting the Pantanal, I stayed in a small wildlife lodge that was famous for huge number of breeding birds in the wet season. In the breeding season there are thousands of colourful storks, herons, egrets and spoonbills all nesting in small trees. The breeding season is during the wet season and as result the ground is flooded. The trees have adapted to having their roots underwater for six months and then being dry for the rest of the year.

To access this spectacular site the lodge had built a raised walkway – c3 metres off the ground and a mile long. We visited in the dry season but there was still huge amount of wildlife around albeit not the breeding birds as described above. We still used the walkway to get to various location as the undergrowth was tricky to walk through. Two of us were watching various wildlife when dusk approached so we started to walk back to lodge with me leading the way.

The walkway is 3 metres off the ground and on either side were trees to 12 to 15 metres high and close to the walkway, so it made a natural tunnel through the forest.

In the fading light I could see something moving about 200 metres away and approaching quickly. When they got to within 50 metres, I realised they were thousands of bats swarming down the walkway to the open forest, they were using this as a natural flight path from their roosting site.

There were thousands of them all flying between one to two metres above the floor of the walkway all coming straight at me. The bats

146

were Bulldog bats with wingspan of around a metre all flying at a rapid pace.

As they approach me, about one metre away, they rose to fly just over my head, some brushing my hair whilst others flew around me at head level.

It was most disconcerting.

I stopped walking, stood and watch them fly above and around me, some only inches from my face. To start with it was scary but once you realise, they were flying around me I just watched the show.

I confess I did flinch on several occasions as it was unsettling seeing them come straight at my face. My mate behind me said "They will not touch you" as I flinched again. I replied, "Easy to say that standing behind me, you try standing here".

The whole fly by lasted c10 minutes and we were told by the owner of lodge that this happens every night and they estimate 20,000 bats fly down the walkway.

It was amazing but a slightly scary spectacle.

Baby bears

I went on a wildlife trip to Romania to see European Brown Bears which we saw several relatively close up.

We stayed in a hunting lodge within a large working forest. Most forests in Eastern Europe are working forests including hunting and timber management. A couple of weeks before we arrived a group of forest workers were clearing an area when a female bear ran out of her den and left behind were three small cubs – around one month old.

One of the forest workers decided to take them home rather than leaving them to die. We were taken to his home a very small house built for forest workers – pretty rough. The bears were now six weeks old and had been bottled fed by the wife of the forest worker and looked to be thriving.

The bears were lovely just like small children. We all had a chance to hold them which was fun. The one I held kept crawling up my body, I didn't like the idea of them crawling on my face due to their 50mm claws (worried about my eyes) so I tried to keep him down except he loved climbing.

They all laughed at me as I tried to manage this baby bear away from my face and eyes.

The idea was to release them back into the forest, but they were imprinted to humans and had little natural training so would not survive back in the wild. They also thought about giving them to a zoo, but these things are 'easier said than done'. Unfortunately, with their rapid growth their future would need to be sorted within three to five months, but I was not hopeful.

I think the forest worker had the 'right intentions but had unfortunately not thought it through'.

39

St Petersburg story of the last Tsar, Rasputin and where was the Tsar buried?

Last Tsar ..... Nicholas 2nd ..... shot 1917

When I visited St Petersburg I was keen to understand the Russian revolution, the last Tsar and Rasputin so I visited many museums, asked lots of questions and read a great book (it was an autobiography of a monk who took high office in Russia, written by himself so the writing was 'raw and not polished' and, at times, boring). It included significant information on Grigori Rasputin and Tsar Nicholas 2nd. He knew Rasputin and the Tsar having had many meetings and conversations about the church and his position within Russian society. His view was that the Tsar was incompetent, vain and detached from his people. He had vast wealth and many 'playthings' whilst majority of Russians led miserable lives. Many other sources appear to support his views.

Even in the 1917 the Tsar had huge power. Even though there was a separate Government it still answered to the Tsar whereas the UK monarch was only a 'figure head' and had little actual power. Power was reinforced by the noblemen as they needed each other to maintain the status quo. Serfdom was officially abolished in Russia in 1861 but took 30 years or so to die out, in comparison, in England, it was over by 1500.

When WW1 started, he made himself Commander in Chief of the armed forces.... but had no military training or natural military skills so it was a disaster, Russia lost battle after battle. Once the revolution had succeeded it 'sued for peace' in 1917.

Nicholas 2nd wife was Alexandra, a strong very determined woman and their eldest son, called Alexei, was a haemophiliac (person who would not stop bleeding if cut).

Faberge museum and Faberge eggs

Yes, beautiful stunning objects but illustrated obnoxious wealth. The Faberge eggs summed up what I felt about the last Tsar.

Beautiful objects that were just a plaything, at Easter, for a few days, then ignored. The eggs were smaller than I thought they would be, about 600 to 800mm high. Each one was different, some had beautiful birds on top others just jewels around them.

One had a small horse and carriage (copy of the Tsar's) with wheels that turned.

You could judge them as either stunning or obnoxious.

Grigori Rasputin .... Russian Mystic ...1869 to 1916 aged 47

There are thousands of stories and rumours about Rasputin, and many would have been exaggerated to make the 'story telling more interesting'...the book I read explained how the basis of these stories are based on facts.

Rasputin was a peasant farmer until the aged of 30 when he discovered God and went on several pilgrimages, lasting months. He claimed he was a Mystic and could help people and even cure them. The rumours and stories, about Rasputin, were so strong the church allowed him to join as a monk even though he had no formal training or education, they 'came under his charm'. But there is 'no smoke without fire' and even, in the book, some of the church leaders who hated him couldn't ignore the stories and rumours as there were so many.

The stories of his powers reached Alexandra, the wife of Nicholas 2nd, who requested a meeting.

Question. Why is Alexandra wanting to meet a monk from peasant stock who looked odd, was dirty and very unpleasant?

This was link to religion and fear..... the very poor and very rich....
both believed in Mystics who could tell them the future or help
make them better or stronger.

The Poor: You can understand they had nothing but 'hope'.

The Rich: They had everything but were terrified they would lose it,
of course, history shows many kings and Tsars were murdered for
power especially amongst family and friends .... you don't know
who to trust.

The rich were and, probably still are, in a constant state of anxiety
so someone who can predict the future, in a positive manner is good
news. Also, they are 'bored' as they have nothing to do all day, they
are even dressed by someone else. It is rumoured that Alexandra
would have her hair combed, every day, for two hours.

Rasputin obviously charmed Nicholas 2nd and especially Alexandra,
gaining trust and power in the household. His biggest asset was to
help Alexei to recover from his illnesses, which were many, and his
haemophilia.

The book claimed that Rasputin worked closely with the Tsar's
doctor and between them they would give Alexei small amount of
poison (not enough to kill him but just to make him unwell for a few
days). So, Rasputin would then predict he would get well in a few
days – to the exact day – and he would support the doctor by saying
he is giving him the right treatment. And, of course, he did get well
....so Rasputin and the doctor were heroes.... but Rasputin being
very clever always came out the biggest hero.

Rasputin loved women and sex, as soon as he walked into a room,
he would check out the ladies. His great 'chat up line' was that as a
Mystic monk he could 'cleanse' you of the devil.... how? You can
guess.

He was famous for sleeping with many of the top noblemen's wives
and possibly Alexandra herself but that is not proven. Of course,

once you have been cleansed you can't tell people especially your husband as the devil will come back. He would also target nuns saving them from the devil.

He also liked to drink and was often very drunk.

Overtime his influence over Alexandra grew especially during WW1 as Nicholas 2nd was away, overseeing the armed forces. Rasputin 'rose to power' through influencing Alexandra which had an impacted on the noblemen and tension grew, until the point when he was murdered in 1916 by a group of young men whose fathers were prominent noblemen.

Rasputin was an interesting character and, if only half the stories were true ...he would be still as interesting.

Yusupov Palace and where Rasputin was murdered

For me this was the highlight of the visit to St Petersburg. The Palace was owned by the richest nobleman in Russia at the time of the last Tsar. The building was interesting and well presented.

BUT the best bit was that Rasputin was 'murdered' in a room at the bottom of the house.

Rasputin was invited to supper with the young nobleman whose parents owned the Palace. He was invited to come for cake and wine, a bit odd as Rasputin was beginning to understand there were 'forces against him'. But he came.

He was served 'wine and cake', the cake had enough poison to kill several men. As expected, he collapsed. The young man went to find his friends who were hiding in other room but as he came back Rasputin attacked him. The young man then shot him twice but instead of falling he staggered out into the garden where he was shot again. They then grabbed him, still alive, and threw him into the nearby river where he drowned.

It was great being in the room where he was killed, yes, it was done up as a museum, but to be in that room, as he was an iconic figure in Russian history.

1917 Revolution

The main focal point of the revolution was in St Petersburg driven by factory workers and Naval men, interestingly the sailors held the key to 'holding the revolution together' as they had guns, and the army didn't want to fight against each other. The key reason for the revolution was that Russia was doing very badly in the war. There was little food and money, yet the rich kept living a 'wealthy lifestyle' which the factory workers and naval men based in the centre of St Petersburg could see.

Lenin was based there and gave many speeches some from his office balcony at 'what is now the political museum', (excellent museum).

When the revolution started the people marched to the Winter Palace, in the centre of St Petersburg, demanding the Tsar to resign and leave St Petersburg. A few days prior to this the Generals had a 'vote of no confidence' in both him leading the army and his overall rule.

So, pressure had built up and he had no option but to leave without a fight.

As the Tsar went willingly from the Palace it was not 'burnt down or ransacked' albeit there was some looting, but this was generally prevented as the police guarded the palace during the uprising. Photographs in the political museum show hundreds of thousands of people in a happy mood marching outside the palace, it was a peaceful take over.

When the elections happened immediately after the revolution, the communist party didn't do so well. Lenin's view was 'if we can't get what we want by peaceful means, we take it by force'.

Hence, the Civil war between 1917 and 1922.

Communist were the Reds and the rest the Whites (group of different political ideas but all apposed communism). The Whites were mainly from the south, Ukraine and the Caucasus and supported by large number of Cossacks from various regions. The Civil war was very bloody and violent against the common people as well as the fighting men, eight million people died.

Of course, Lenin and the communist party won.

Lenin died in 1924 and Stalin took over until he died in 1953.

Yekaterinburg – city where the Tsar and family were taken and killed

26 Hours by train from Moscow, situated on the east side of the Ural Mountains and 24 miles (40km) inside of Asia. The city began in 1723 to make iron and steel and then to build weapons, cannons and big guns for the Russian military.

All the key raw materials for steel making and manufacturing are all available in proximity, but I asked our guide "How do you get the stuff to St Petersburg main military base, its hundreds of miles away on very poor roads?".

Answer. "By boat"

"Yes, but the water freezes in the winter and in the summer the water levels will drop so it is difficult to carry such heavy loads and the rivers flow south and not to St Petersburg". I replied

"Correct. So, they only moved their output just after the spring flood, once the water volume had died down from the rapid thaw but there was sufficient water in the system. The boat men had to try and pick the right moment to sail from Yekaterinburg to Moscow and St Petersburg".

In the Spring thaw Russian waterways are often interlinked and where there is no natural link, they have built canals. In effect, they move one year's full production in a few weeks....and then build up stock for next year. When you compare it to our modern factories where we run on the basis of 'stock just in time' it is a different timeframe and attitude.

The city is still a major mining, steel making and manufacturing centre. However, its latest 'toy' is the S400 missile defensive system judged by many to be the best in the world. It currently makes Russia a lot of money and Turkey (member of NATO) bought it in 2019 much to the fury of the USA.

City – It was great to visit a normal city with very few tourists. It was basic, slightly dirty, a bit grim, but not too bad and you could live there, similar to Sheffield.

I went on a long walk, by myself, and stopped at a coffee shop, full of local people. Coffee was good and cake ok. I think I made the wrong choice rather than it was poor as other people's cakes looked great. (I ordered off a menu by guessing and pointing at a Russian word, you couldn't see samples of the cakes).

What was interesting is that ALL the men, young and old, were very polite to their girlfriend or wife. They ALL help them with their chair and ALL help the ladies with their coat...not like us.

Yekaterinburg is famous for being where the last Tsar and his family were murdered.

The Tsar was held in the centre of the city in a large, nice house, so well looked after, with servants etc. There are stories of him living the simple life, for example cutting logs for winter, but this is just political propaganda by the pro Tsar camp.

They were killed on the night of the 17th July 1918 (late at night or very early next day) and shot in the basement. This was during the Civil war and the White army was approaching the city, so the order was given......probably from Moscow but no evidence survives. The communist party has always positioned it, that a 'drunk officer' killed them without due authority.

The house where they were killed has been destroyed so that it couldn't become a 'rallying cry' for the Whites. In 2003 a church was built next to this house to 'mark the place'. All very interesting ....and in a built-up area with people going about their normal activities.

So, where are they buried?

We drove 20 miles outside the city to two burial sites;

1. Official one.

   It was believed, and still is the official position, that they were buried in some old lime pits, we were shown these pits. The Tsar and his family were burnt and then covered in lime, to dissolve the bones, and then buried here.

   Next to the site, in 2000, a new church and monastery were developed with many monks staying there. The Russian Orthodox Church seems to 'have a thing' about the old Tsar and latching onto it, almost going back a full circle, the 'church identifying with the White side' in the civil war. The church, of course, was banned under the communist rule and in the last c30 years has become more prominent, in the rural areas away from the rule of Moscow the church continued surreptitiously.

   To me, it seems a dangerous game of modern politics.

2. Unofficial but the most likely site.

   In the 1960's some civil servants were working in the area and studying the records of the soldiers involved in their murder especially the officer (the army always keep records). They found a small bit about how the bodies were moved and buried several miles away under some old railway sleepers, an old trick to stop wolves digging up the bodies.

Senior Management told them to ignore it, but when they retired, and the political environment had changed they went back to their research. After a few months they believe they have found the 'proper burial site'.

The church and the Government refuses to believe it and continue to resist having an independent DNA test on the bones discovered. Given the church has built a large church and monastery, on the official site, they are not too keen to say they are in the wrong place.

The guide had a PHD in history so did his father and grandfather (history runs in the family) AND was very knowledgeable and enthusiastic. They believe that the unofficial site is more accurate.

40

Who is the top predator in the Taiga Forest, Brown Bear or Gray Wolf?

Background

I went wildlife viewing in a remote hide in 'no man's land' on the Finnish Russian border.

Finland and Russia have had many land disputes and invasions over the last 300 years with Russia usually being the aggressor. Immediately after WW2 Russia made a land grab but under pressure from the west this was resisted. An agreement was made to have a 'gap' or 'no man's land' between the two countries, running the entire length of the border and between three and 10 miles wide. No one is allowed in, no farming, no hunting, nothing so wildlife flourish and the habitat has been restored. The exception is a few photographic hides where wildlife enthusiasts can visit.

I spent six nights, often alone, in the hide from 6pm to 8am, all night. The hide is 120 miles south of the Arctic circle and because I visited in mid-June it was nearly 24-hour daylight albeit at times gloomy.

To encourage wildlife the owner leaves nuts and a dead sheep for the bears to feed on. I had excellent sightings of Brown Bears, Gray Wolves and Wolverine.

Young wolf and Alpha male

The hide sits in a large wolf territory and the pack is usually seen every three weeks or so. I was lucky to have them in the area, so I watched them most nights.

In Europe wolf packs tend to be quite small usually between three and eight animals. I identified the alpha male and three adolescent wolves, one of which, was trying to be adopted by this pack.

10 miles to the north was another wolf pack but the alpha male and female had both been shot by poachers a few months before. As a result, the pack had dispersed, and a young wolf had appeared looking to be accepted. Usually, the resident alpha male would either chase it away or kill it, however, given the circumstances he was more tolerant. The background to this was pieced together by the owner of the hides and what we had witnessed as the young wolf had only just appeared. Of course, it is only our interpretation of events.

Great bit of behaviour

The hide I was sitting in had a small pond, in front, and then a large clearing flanked on both sides by forest. At 1 am the alpha male emerged from the forest, his thick coat was light brown, like a ghost drifting through the trees. He had an aura, a presence bigger than the animal.

Following five metres behind, looking downtrodden, was the young wolf from the other pack. I knew this as I had shared photographs with the owner the previous day as we discussed the situation, confirming it was a new animal in the territory.

The pair slowly wandered into the clearing, the young animal keeping his distance and head down looking downtrodden. From the opposite side of the clearing a large male Brown Bear appeared from the forest, upon seeing the wolves the bear became very alert and anxious. After a few minutes he started to move away and then quickly moved to 'top gear' charging directly away from the hide. Bears can run at 30 miles an hour and he was off at top speed.

At this point the alpha male and young wolf exchanged looks and with a nod from the alpha male the young wolf followed the bear at full speed. After 10 minutes the young wolf came back, clearly pleased with himself, holding himself in full posture.

He came straight up to the alpha male looking for approval, which was given by a 'clear nod of the head'. At that point the young wolf laid flat on his back with legs in the air submitting to the male, who sniffed him and then walk off. The young wolf leapt to his feet and followed the alpha male but this time very close behind him, but always behind him, with a positive stance with his head held high.

Whether he was now accepted? No idea, but interesting behaviour.

Top predator

Even though brown bears are at least 10 times heavier than wolves, wolves are the top predator.

Wolves are much quicker and nimbler than the bear so will get behind it and 'bite it on the bum', this can go on and on and if the bear stays and fights the wolf will eventually kill the bear by wearing it down. Of course, if the bear hits the wolf with its giant paw and powerful muscles it will kill the wolf, so the wolf can't make a mistake. Most of the time the wolf will win.

41

Have you ever seen a hunt whilst on safari?

This is a common question people ask me.

Not in the classical view of a Lion taking down a Zebra as often seen on TV, but I have witnessed a chase.

African Painted Dogs (also called hunting dogs)

On my overland trip between South Africa and Uganda the truck stopped at Chobe River National Park Botswana for several nights.

We had a dawn trip, into the reserve. The safari vehicle worked its' way slowly alongside the river and floodplain, which was on the right, and open dry woodland covering the hills on the left. The floodplain held a scattered herd of Impalas calmly feeding. Impalas are antelope, slender and agile with the ability to leap a distance of ten metres and three metres high.

From around a bend a small pack of hunting dogs came into view – four adults and ten puppies. The dogs are long limbed with a lean strong body and large ears. They stand around 1.3 metres high and look ferocious. They maintained a steady pace walking along the floodplain and at times came very close to the vehicle in a calm and measured manner albeit the puppies were always shielded from us.

Without warning or command communication (to us) two adult dogs set off at a canter, one went straight towards the Impalas whilst the other went to the right in a large circular motion. There was uproar and chaos within the Impala herd all sprinting off in different directions and all calling out warning noises. The dogs picked on certain individuals for a brief period and then realising it was not a weak or old they quickly switched their attention to the next one.

When a particular Impala was being focussed on, it changed its gait jumping higher whilst simultaneously kicking out both front and back legs parallel to its underbody and running at speed. This seems an inefficient and clumsy method but what it is saying to the Dogs – 'I am young and fit, and you can't catch me'.

The Dogs focused on five or six different Impalas with no luck and the Impalas moved off the floodplain into the forest. The Dogs came back to the group and carried on walking along the floodplain as if nothing had happened.

42

Have you ever seen a bird of prey making a kill?

Yes, several times:

European Goshawk

Background

We had a family holiday in Denmark. Why Denmark?

We had a family meeting with my children, Tom (then aged 11) and Jess (eight), asking what they wanted to do on our next year's family holiday, any requests.

Tom immediately said "I want to go to Lego Land"

"Yes, but we can do the one in Surrey on a day out" I replied

"NO Lego Land in Denmark the 'real' one" he replied at which point Jess said "Me too"

You asked the question, so you live with the answer, we had two weeks in Denmark.

We first stayed in a forest camp, in the centre of the main island allowing us to have day trips out to Lego Land, the beach etc. The second week we travelled overland to Copenhagen staying in family hotels whilst exploring more of the country and staying three nights at the capital. Denmark has some wonderful named Towns – the best is Middelfart – the kids loved that when they found it on the map. So, on the way back from Copenhagen we 'had to' stay there.

Sarah booked a hotel which looked very nice but more expensive than usual, but as we had kept within our general budget throughout the holiday, so we decided to go for it. We found the Hotel on the outskirts of the town. A large stately home with extensive grounds and a very long access road!!!

"Bloody hell Sarah what have you booked us? How much? Is that rate per person NOT the total cost for all of us?"

"It will be right" she replied slightly nervously.

It was a huge wonderful stately home which made its money on 'fine dining' – the price of a full evening meal, for one, was nearly double the cost of the room. That night we had 'fish and chips' in Middelfart. Kids had a great time making loud rude noises – much to their amusement.

After breakfast we strolled down a very long lawn at the back of the house to the sea and then turned right along the beach where we found a small hill fort. The fort was built in c700 for the local regional king, all that was left was large earth mounds.

Whilst standing on one of these mounds I heard several alarm calls and 50 or so Jackdaws all flying panicking into the sky. Looking around, I saw a Goshawk with its talons facing forward thump into a Jackdaw no more than three metres away. It was a loud thud.

Both birds tumbled out of the sky. The Jackdaw laid flat on its back looking dead or unconscious.

At this point I realised it was a Juvenile Goshawk (it had Juvenile feathers) as it just sat on the ground less than a metre from the Jackdaw not knowing what to do next.... it looked at the bird.... looked at me...looked around and just sat there.

This being July I assume it was one of its first hunting missions whilst still being fed by the parents. The Goshawk looked wonderful – even though it was a youngster it was powerful and with big eyes.

I didn't move and I watched it for 5 minutes or so, at which point the Jackdaw lifted its head, shook himself and flew off, much to the amazement of both the Goshawk and me.

Sparrowhawk taking a starling

My favourite wildlife reserve, in the UK, is Leighton Moss which has a large Starling murmuration over a huge reedbed. In late Autumn thousands and thousands of Starlings will roost in the reserve and often congregate near one of the remote hides.

I love sitting there in the low evening light watching them fly in huge circles. Of course, that many Starlings means food for the local Sparrowhawk population. That evening I witnessed six kills, four being plucked out of the reeds and two in mid-air.

The one which I remember most and still disturbs me was a bird being taken 3 metres from me in mid-air and I could clearly hear the Starling scream. And, unfortunately It was still screaming as the Sparrowhawk flew off with it.

43

How was the Maldives formed?

I loved physical geography at school and on my subsequent trips around the world I would analyse the landscape to try and understand how it was formed and shaped by natural processes.

Discovering how the Maldives were created 'blew my mind'. The power of nature and time.

The Maldives are made up of vast coral reef atolls that sit on old volcanic rocks 2,300 metres underneath the Maldives. The 2,300 metres difference is made up of sand from old coral that has been worn down and built up over millions of years. The Maldives are c500 miles long with two parallel atolls with over 1,000 islands, of which, the vast majority are sand islands forming part of the coral reef atoll.

There are three types of Coral Reefs

- Barrier Reefs – growing on shallow water in the sea or ocean – can be 200 miles from land such as Australia Great Barrier Reef.
- Fringe Reefs – growing in shallow water next to the land such as Galapagos
- Atoll Reefs – often isolated in the ocean, Maldives is a typical example.

How are Maldives Atolls made?

- Originally the Maldives were a long line of volcanoes formed millions of years ago and the tops of the volcanoes were above sea level, often by several thousand feet.
- Around the coast on the edge of the land – Fringe reefs started to grow.

- Over time via natural erosion the volcanoes were worn down and sank below the sea.
- The reef is constantly being eaten away by fish such as Wrasse that bite chunks off, chewing the coral whilst eating the alga which grows inside and then splitting out the leftover rock which had been chewed into sand.
- During this process the growth of the Fringe Reef more or less kept pace with the sinking volcanic rock and the build-up of sand, so it stays just below the surface of the sea. Overtime the sea level will also fluctuate due to climate change such as 'ice ages' however, these changes have been slow enough, for the reef to respond and not to be wiped out.
- So, when the volcanic peaks disappeared you are left with huge circular reefs with sea water in the centre. These new atoll reefs are formed from the old fringe reefs that originally surrounded the volcano. The sea lagoons in the centre of the atoll reef can stretch up to 40 miles across.
- As the volcanic peaks are worn further below the surface the sand and grit deposited by the fish increases supporting the reef above.
- In the Maldives these processes have been going on for millions of years and the sand deposit has built up – the original volcanic land is 2,300 metres below sea level.
- One side of the atoll reef directly faces the open ocean and the land falls away very rapidly – within 100 metres of the reef the sea can be 400 metres deep – 1 mile from land it can 2,000 metres deep. Whilst snorkelling on the outer reefs you can clearly see the sea falling away into the gloom. Snorkelling along this line you can sometime see very large fish, dolphins and sharks.
- As the land and sea changes the atoll reef often expands so there is an outer reef and an inner reef though the distance between them, is only small, usually less than two hundred metres. On the inside of the inner reef the sand accumulates and spreads out in shallow lagoons protected from the open ocean by the outer reefs. As a result, they form huge shallow lagoons, 0.6 to 2 metres deep, the sunlight reflects from the white sand through the clear sea producing a turquoise colour – stunning.

- Sometimes the reef is broken and sea currents running through them, so the lagoons are much deeper and form small seas.

Nature and natural processes have created amazing landscapes – beautiful and stunning.

44

Street food .... I have never tried

I usually happy to try anything once, except!!!

Grilled Rats

I was walking through a small market in Luang Prabang, Laos, looking at the various foods on sales, mainly fruit and veg with some meat like chicken etc.

I then came across a small stall offering.... grilled rats.

In a basket were four grilled rats with their head, tail, legs and feet still in place. The rats had been gutted and then grilled.

I was shocked and felt sad for the people who could only afford this type of meat.

I quickly decided I was NOT going to try it.

Deep fried Tarantulas

During a long road trip, within Cambodia, we stopped at a small village for a comfort break.

The area is sparsely populated so the village has become the main stopping place for lorries, businessmen and locals travelling along this road from Laos to Phnom Penh. The village has become famous within Cambodia for selling fresh locally produced fruit and vegetables but it's other specialism is farming and selling 'deep fried Tarantulas'.

The Tarantulas were fried whole, they have a chunky body about 75mm wide and still had their legs and fangs.

The villagers also like to deep fry Cockroaches and other insects.

Again, these didn't appeal.

Fly burgers

Lake Malawi and the surrounding areas support a huge breeding population of flies. In season the flies swarm in massive numbers above the lake forming huge black clouds swirling around.

Certain areas around the lake have significant levels of poverty and locals take advantage of this considerable amount of protein by collecting the flies in fine nets. They then squash them down into burgers patties and grill them.

No not for me.

Bottle of wine with dead snakes in them

Drinking a glass of white wine which you know have been poured from a bottle that holds a dead snake is not something I would care to sample.

I might be a white, middle-class westerner but if it doesn't appeal to me, so I don't see the point of trying it.

However, in the Far East they appear to sell in large numbers so they must have a market.

45

Buddha teeth important relic

I am not a religious person, but I find it interesting the emotional impact religion has on people as well as the physical show of support (temples, churches etc) for their chosen religion reflecting their culture and history.

Buddhism has always interested me as a religion that is passive and reflective founded by Siddhartha Gautama in Nepal in 5th century B.C.

By chance rather than forward planning I have visited all three temples where it is alleged that one of Buddha's teeth are held. These temples are some of the most important Buddhist temples in the world.

Sri Lanka – Kandy – Temple of the Tooth

The main religion in Sri Lanka is Buddhism whilst in India Hinduism dominates with a small important Buddhist populated in Northern India and Nepal where it originated from.

Inside the Royal Palace complex in Kandy, a small town which used to be the main power base of Sri Lanka 500 years ago, is the Temple of the Tooth. Hundreds of thousands of people come to pray every year including many international Buddhists.

The Temple was relatively small with lovely gold Buddhas statues but what was brilliant was the atmosphere, local people praying and worshiping the 'tooth' which is kept out of sight in a gold box. You can't see the tooth so no one, apart from the high priest, knows if it exists, however, in religion belief is often more important than reality.

Even though it is a popular place to worship it was not crowded and you could see and feel the atmosphere of dedication and belief.

I don't believe in religion but the impact on these people was powerful, very moving.

Mongolia – Ulaanbaatar – Gandan Khiid Monastery

The monastery was a large complex of small temples and buildings with large numbers of young monks milling around. Plus, there were local people coming to pray and giving their respects.

Buddhas tooth was tucked away in a small building but didn't appear, to me, to be the main central point for religious activities.

As we walked around, we noticed a large group of older monks gathering inside a temple with numerous prayer wheels. The old monks started chanting and walking around the prayer wheels rotating them as they moved and then they sat in the middle chanting whilst meditating. We were lucky as there is no set time for this activity it happens when the monks feel it is appropriate.

There were only five of us and the only foreigners in the complex so the local guide asked if we could watch? We were in luck as they invited us in, and we could walk around the group but were not allowed to stop and must keep going in a clockwise direction.

Majority of monks became so involved in the chanting they appeared to be a deep trance. We stayed for a while slowly walking round and round the group.

Singapore – Buddha Tooth Relic Temple

The story goes that Buddhas teeth were scattered to different parts of the world where Buddhism is worshipped as foreigners were invading northern India.

One of these teeth arrived in Singapore and is displayed behind closed doors in the Buddha Tooth Relic Temple.

Personally, I found this temple soulless without atmosphere.

46

Inside out Zoo

I travelled with my wife around New Zealand for three months. I was particularly interested in how the modern world had impacted the environment especially the flora and fauna.

Summary of how the fauna and flora, in NZ, has developed overtime:

- 100 million years ago New Zealand was isolated from all other land masses.
- 30 million years ago, in the rest of the world, mammals evolved and ruled the world developing predators such as wild cats, rats, stoats etc. Other mammals and birds adjusted to living alongside them to survive or were wiped out.
- NZ was 'bypassed' by mammals and didn't develop any land predators and the only 2 birds of prey, one of which, a large eagle that preyed on the giant Mao birds (both now extinct).
- As a result, NZ land birds evolved to have no predators so often lost the power of flight – 'why do you need to fly if you don't have to flee a predator'. They also became very tame and curious coming towards you to investigate rather than fleeing.
- Due to this isolation NZ developed a vast range of endemic plants and tree life, such as ferns as well as a large range of endemic birds of which a large proportion had become flightless or had very weak flights.
- Maori people invaded c800 years ago, but the main damage was done by the Europeans who very quickly settled in the country c150 years ago.
- Unfortunately, the Europeans brought the rat (ship rats get everywhere) cats and dogs, as pets, as well as pigs, goats and rabbits as food. Unfortunately, these escaped and developed wild feral breeding colonies especially the rabbit, which breed like

rabbits!! To control the escaped rabbit population the Europeans introduced stoats.

- Europeans also brought Possums from Australia for fur farming, again many escaped and now the population is estimated to be over 80 million – unfortunately they sit and eat all the leaves from a certain area before moving on but by then they have destroyed all the trees. In Australia, the native trees have weak acid which is stimulated by browsing so after a short period the Possums, if they want to eat, are forced to move on.
- The native birds, lizards etc were 'hammered' by these introduced predators and a significant number have become extinct or reduced to very small populations often in the low hundreds.
- A good example, of what the country is facing is Fiordland. It looks like true wilderness – it 800 miles long and 90 miles wide with NO roads or tracks and NO buildings or human settlements. The area is mountainous with large forests that are a mixture of native and foreign invasive plants – it looks like wilderness – however, it is a veneer.

The entire countryside is overrun with stoats and rats, so the native bird life has nearly been destroyed.

We sailed around the fiords for six days and had several walks deep into the forest – hard going as there are no tracks, but it was great to be inside the forest. But there was NO BIRD life and very quiet. Over several hours I saw one bird. The silence was amazing – no human noises but also no bird/animal noises – worrying.

If the wildlife of remote Fiordland is knackered, then the whole of NZ is knackered.

What can be done?

Island sanctuaries

They have developed island sanctuaries especially if they are situated many miles from the mainland. The authorities clear the island of feral predators such as rats and let the native birds and animals survive, including re-introduction programmes. For example; The Kakapo a large nocturnal parrot, which is flightless, is now confined to four small offshore islands where previously they occurred throughout the mainland. Unfortunately, they are tame and inquisitive so when approached by a feral cat they would go towards it as curious and then, of course, cats do what cats do.

The population was reduced to 18 birds, but now due to protection on these islands, the population has increased to 252. Due to the vulnerability of these birds and the possibility of introducing feral predators these islands are closed to the public.

However, some sanctuaries are open to the public such as ULVA island off Stewart Island and we visited several times. It is a beautiful island with native trees and more importantly many native birds and animals including breeding NZ Fur Seals. Even though it is six miles from Stewart Island rats occasionally swim across the sea, so the situation is constantly monitored. If a breeding rat population was an established, it would destroy the native bird population within a couple of years.

Mass Poisoning – 1060

This is very controversial. 1060 is a poison developed by the government that, it is believed, kills all the introduced predators as well as 90% of the local wildlife. The theory is that the leftover native population re-starts a natural breeding programme and overtimes re-populates the area.

We stopped at an area, remote and sparsely populated, where the Government was planning, in the next few months, to drop 1060 by planes and helicopters over thousands and thousands of acres of land. But there were still people living in the bush. They were told, just close your windows and stay inside for two days and don't drink outside water for two months. As you can guess they were not happy and there were lots of protest posters.

A significant proportion of conservationists are not convinced this is the best way, but unfortunately, no one has come up with the perfect solution.

Inside out Zoo

Another technique used to conserve the native birds and animals such as lizards on the mainland is to build huge enclosures and eradicate all introduced predators and stock it with native birds etc. Some of the birds will be local and feed in the surrounding areas and use the area for safe nesting sites.

In other countries, they have zoos with wildlife from other countries and fence them off to protect them and the surrounding environment. In NZ, the zoo protects native wildlife, inside the zoo and prevents feral creatures trying to get in.

We visited one of these 'inside out Zoos' near Dunedin. The security was 'unreal' a fence that was 5 metres high and curved outwards, to stop animals climbing up the wall, and covered with a mass of barbed wire. A 20-metre strip of land next to the wall was stripped bare, so animals could not use the vegetation to climb up and jump over. It looked very much like a Concentration Camp, we visited in Poland, from the WW2.

Once inside it was excellent – lots of native birds and animals as well as information on their lifestyle and the challenges they face in modern NZ.

47

Unusual animals and their environment

Southern Brown Kiwi – New Zealand

Kiwi is the National bird of New Zealand but is very hard to see/ find, the vast majority of New Zealanders have never seen one. On both North and South Island there are only c10,000 left due to into introduced predators. On Stewart Island there are c20,000 and is therefore the best place to see one.

Unfortunately, as they are very shy and nocturnal it meant that, after several attempts, I managed only to hear but not see one.

Fortunately, I had done my research prior to our trip.

There is a famous David Attenborough programme where he watched a Kiwi on the beach, at night, eating sea lice from seaweed. The guy who introduced David Attenborough to Kiwis now runs similar boat trips, so we went to the same beach and were able to watch three different kiwis.

First you get a boat to this deserted island, about 15 miles away which takes an hour – you then walk for ½ hour through the trees in the dark before reaching the beach. Luckily, we didn't have to wait long before they turned up, we had several excellent views in the moon light.

And, then the walk back – with a boat trip at night with all the stars out – an excellent trip.

Glow worm caves – New Zealand

Lake Te Anau is a huge lake that splits Fiordland from the rest of South Island – it is pretty, but I didn't rave about it. I found it frustrating as beyond the lake is wilderness but on our side of the lake were rows of motels – all a bit plastic and touristy.

In the small town was a great café/shop – a hunting and fishing shop with the café showing hunting pictures of dead animals – the food was excellent – however, Sarah (my wife) didn't like looking at dead animals whilst she was eating her dead animal for lunch!!!

The highlight were the Glow Worm caves.

We caught a boat trip for hour across the lake through a series of small islands and channels. We then entered the cave, which was huge. To start with we walked into the cave for 600 metres and then had a small boat ride deep into the cave. At the end of the cave the guide turned the lights out – the sight was amazing thousands upon thousands of stars shining in the dark accept they were not stars but NZ Glow Worms – these are unique to NZ.

All through the cave system were Glow Worms but the biggest density was towards the end – they like dark and wet places to breed and feed. I would estimate these Glow Worms are three to four times brighter than similar ones I have seen before in Europe and Asia.

It was an amazing spectacle, living in dark caves in huge numbers shining brightly.

The glow worms feed on insects blown into the cave. To help attract insects they glow in the dark and often hang, sometimes feet, from the ceiling glowing as much as they can to make themselves stand out and be attractive.

The whole experience was excellent – the talk about the Glow Worms at the beginning, the trip into the cave and the boat trip.

Giant Anteater – Brazil – Serra da Canastra National Park

This was poor rural Brazil.

The village had around 300 houses with one main dirt road that finished at the edge of the village and turned into bush – no barrier just the end of the road. The village had a nice atmosphere, we stayed in a basic but clean hotel surround by poor quality housing with friendly people and lots of dogs.

We had a full day in the National Park which was up a mountain with flat tops rather than jagged high peaks. The habitat was dry grassland, which was low in nutrients, so the density of wildlife is low.

The morning was slow with only a distant view of an Anteater, but we had a great piece of good fortune. We stopped to look at a couple of Pampas Deer which are very rare because of hunting. We decided to stalk the deer to get a photo when one of our group, who was behind me and slightly to the left, stumbled on a sleeping Giant Anteater!!

First thing I knew there was a Giant Anteater slowly running pass me six metres to the left.

The animal didn't look worried, so I ran parallel to it getting some nice pictures. The animal kept going slowly and without being bothered about me so I ran in front/slightly to the right side of her (to the side so not to worry her – she was big – at least two metres long so obviously a female, males are much smaller) and got some great photos of the front of the animal rather than just her backside.

She did lift her head up and have a quick look at me to check me out (I knelt to the floor in a passive manner) and then she moved off slightly more to the left but obviously not concerned as her overall demeanour was calm.

They can be aggressive with very powerful front claws used to tear open termite mounts. They have in the past killed people if disrupted or hassled. For 15 minutes or so I kept pace with her watching her behaviour for signs of aggression as well as studying her.

When we were in the Pantanal, we spotted a female Giant Anteater who got extremely worried about our vehicle and attacked the wheels and side of the truck. It was a 'full on' assault using her 150mm claws on her front legs slashing the truck. Amazing and very dangerous.

Luckily on the mountain tops I had 'read' her behaviour correctly.

Greater Adjutants – India

In 2000 I visited Kaziranga national park in Assam, India. The park is huge, one of the largest in India and lies in the flood plain of the Brahmaputra River, one of the great rivers of the world.

I was lucky to find a Great Adjutant bird. A huge ugly bird looking like death, a bit like a dirty and even uglier African Marabou stork.

What makes it special? It is one of the rarest birds in the world and has an interesting history and relationship with man. It was estimated that the world population, in 2000, was less than 100, of course, there could be populations in remote areas that have not been identified.

It was originally a common bird during the British Empire and was widespread in the slums of Calcutta. It is a scavenger with an interesting palate and very strong constitution eating anything that is dead or waste products especially in human slums.

Greater Adjutant is an English name and is derived from their stiff military style gait when walking similar to an Adjutant in the British army (staff officer).

It is not a shy bird and likes to live close to humans and over the last few hundred years have developed the habit of nesting close to villages. Unfortunately, they are a messy and smelly bird leaving lots of dropping and leftover food scattered around the trees they have nested in. In addition, villagers thought they represented evil, and death so would often destroy the nesting sites.

Overtime the population crashed to less than 100, in 2000.

Wildlife conservationists started a campaign to explain to villagers that it is a very rare bird with a very limited world breeding population, literally in their back gardens. In general, villagers have responded to this message, taking pride in the rare bird and now protect it and their nests.

It is now estimated the population is around 1,000.

The rarest bird I have seen is the Brazilian Merganser with an estimated population of less than 50 in 2008, again through wildlife protection of its habitat the population is now estimated to be c250.

Hoatzin Bird – Amazon Rainforest

Whilst paddling in a small boat through small creeks within the Amazon rainforest I came across a small group of Hoatzin birds. It is the size of a large pheasant and most odd looking with bits of hair sticking out of its head. The chicks have claws on its wings and use these to help it climb through the branches – quite pre-historic!!

It is unique being the only bird of its species.

It feeds mainly on leaves and digests its food like cattle using bacterial fermentation process in its gut to break down the green matter. The side effect of this is that local people call it the stink bird!!!

Due to its diet and subsequent huge gut compared to the rest of its body it doesn't fly much just walking through the branches living a quiet sedentary lifestyle and when spotted it often just looks back at you.

Unlike cattle the flesh of the Hoatzin bird has a nasty taste so is rarely preyed upon especially by local tribes, so the population is steady and is estimated at c10,000.

A great bird.

Leopard Tortoise – South Africa – Bontebox National Park

I visited the national park to see Bontebox Hartebeest which is a very attractive animal. Unfortunately, the world population is only c500 because their preferred habitat is grassy plains in the southern areas of South Africa. As a result of white man's occupation of South Africa these fertile plains were heavily farmed, and the population crashed due to loss of habitat and hunting for food.

Prior to my visit I did my research and discovered the park allowed you to walk in certain areas as there are no large predators. I decided to walk alongside the river, at dawn, to watch for birds and animals.

However, I also read it was heavily populated with Puff Adders, a highly venomous snake that is reported to kill c32,000 people a year in Africa.

Puff Adders are 1.3 to 2 metre long and thick as a 'man's arm'.

It's preferred hunting method is to lie in wait, highly camouflaged and ambush any prey that come too close. Unfortunately, they often lie on tracks or pathways keeping completely still, even if you are very close, and being camouflaged people often stand on them. I was fully aware of this and took my time walking through long grass on a vague track alongside the thickly vegetated riverbank.

After a couple of miles taking my time watching the birds and looking out for snakes, I spotted a colourful bird high in the trees whilst still moving forward. Still looking up I froze in mid step at the apex of the movement.

I froze – for many seconds and started to 'sweat and feeling hot and uncomfortable – heart pumping' – I knew something was wrong.

I had NOT seen anything just froze by instinct.

I feared I was going to step on a Puff Adder.

I slowly lowered my head – but could not see anything so I slowly move my foot backwards to reveal a Leopard Tortoise.

Very relieved and after calming down I had a good look. Leopard Tortoise are attractively marked and a lovely animal.

I still don't know how I knew it was there – but very glad it was not a Puff Adder.

I did see a Puff Adder on my trip, whilst in the Namibian Desert, as I got out of my tent in the middle of the night for a pee, luckily it was 10 metres away on the sand lit up by the full moon.

Hummingbirds everywhere – I could and did sit for hours watching them

It is estimated there are 330 different species of Hummingbirds – USA have 10 – Mexico 20 – Ecuador have at least 200.

I was bird watching in the tropical cloud forest in the Andes mountains between 1,300 to 3,000 metres. The Hummingbirds were everywhere in the forest and open scrubland.

Every place we stayed or visited would have hummingbird feeders which attracted them in large numbers. My favourite place was a very rustic forest lodge where we slept in huts and had supper in a central dining hall. I think my garden hut was in better condition however, the location was excellent.

The dining room had a flat roof, and you could walk out onto it, it had four large posts and a roof on top as being the cloud forest it rains a lot. At each corner and in the middle were masses of Hummingbird feeders.

I sat for hours, by myself, watching the birds flying around – they flew like missiles, very straight and fast, most of time flying within the enclosure. On several occasions I thought they would fly into me being so close often brushing my hair or skin with their wing feathers. There were always birds at the feeders but at its peak they could be c40 flying around – a mass of wings and missiles – and stunning colours.

48

Buildings with atmosphere

Angkor Wat – Cambodia

This Hindu temple was built in the 12th century as part of the wider South Indian Empire and was then later converted to Buddhism. It was abandoned in the 16th century and reclaimed by the tropical rainforest. One of the temples still has huge trees growing through the building.

Angkor Wat is a very famous and well-known historical landmark, well documented in travel and historical books. It has unfortunately now become very popular with tourists especially in and around the main temple area.

Pre-dawn, on our first day, we went to watch the sunrise whilst standing near the 'Reflection Pool' in front of the main temple. It was stunning. We were, of course, with several hundred other people however there was a lovely peaceful atmosphere. During this visit I noticed that the walkways surrounding the main temple seemed to be open, so I suggested that pre-dawn the next day we visit the far side of the complex. Walking through the passages of Angkor Wat, lit only by moon light felt 'surreal'. Tom and I stopped at the far end of the temple in a large courtyard, where we sat and watched dawn arriving. We were the only people in the whole complex and we both felt a 'real sense of power and presence', it was a very special place.

That afternoon we visited with several hundred other travellers, in the full heat of the day, it just didn't feel the same.

Catholic Church – Quito, Ecuador

The church was stunningly beautiful with the walls covered in gold and many ornate statues.

The most interesting but also most depressing part were two huge paintings by the Jesuits, Catholics who believed that if you didn't live a 'good religious life' you went to hell and damnation. The paintings showed 'white foreign men' going upwards to heaven and the 'coloured local indigenous people' going down to hell. Both pictures showed the people in hell being tortured such as being burnt alive and eaten by devils.

I found the paintings very sad; they reflected the colonisation of South America and other places. Religion being used as a tool for maintaining power and exploitation.

It gave the church a sombre atmosphere. A huge contrast between the beautiful surroundings and my interpretation of how religion could potentially be used in a negative way.

South America is a melting pot of groups of people from around the world. The local indigenous people, which are in the minority, are wonderful they are very small and very wide almost square like, and very friendly.

Borobudur Temple, central Java – Indonesia

On the way home from our gap year in Australia in 1983 we went overland through Bali and Java.

We visited Borobudur temple one of the largest and greatest Buddhist temples in the world dating from 8th century. Borobudur temple in central Java was the first major historical building outside the UK I have visited. I confess I was naïve about the history of South Asia as we were only taught about British and European history at school and my natural curiosity majored on the WW2.

To see a building that large and stylish with dozens of large Buddha statues enclosed within stupas with lace stonework so that you could see inside was amazing.

We visited during the monsoon season and as a result had the place to ourselves. However, once on top of the temple – which is huge and stands on 3 large tiers forming a pyramid – the rain stopped, and we could appreciate the stillness and peace of the surroundings. To think this was built 1,200 years ago, before most of the major buildings in the UK were even considered, was inspiring.

Hampton Court, UK

Built in the early 1500's and Henry VIII favoured residence.

Between 1500 and 1760 Hampton Court was favoured by various monarchs and many alterations were made but the Chapel and the corridor leading to the Chapel remain from the time of Henry VIII. I found it astonishing that I could walk in the middle of the same corridor that Henry VIII did nearly 500 years before. I was so taken by this I kept going back and re-visiting it.

From 1760 the monarchs moved to central London and so the palace was neglected until it was saved by Queen Victoria and opened to the public.

We stayed in a flat within the Hampton Court complex for 4 days and were allowed to walk around the empty courts in the evenings. I felt a 'real sense of history and presence' within its walls.

Jeronimos Monastery – Lisbon

I found the inside of this Monastery overwhelming – the size of the building and the volume of the decorations – the gold, the colour, the glitter, the paintings – huge numbers all packed into this vast building. It took my breath away.

Without name dropping I have been to both the Vatican and Sistine Chapel, Florence art galleries and museums etc but this Monastery had a much greater impact – I couldn't leave, it was so impressive.

Dolmabahce Palace – Istanbul, Turkey

At school, in history lessons, we didn't cover or learn about the Ottoman Empire, apart from it being on the side of the Germans during the First World War which contributed to its demise. As a result, I never had a feel for how important and powerful it was.

Dolmabahce Palace was built by the Sultan, on the Bosporus straits, as a statement of his wealth and power.

It certainly achieved that. It is an enormous complex with the highlight being the 'Ceremonial Hall' which is huge and stunningly colourful with a mixture of designs reflecting the influence of the Middle East and Europe. The hall seems to encapsulate the status of the empire portraying its power and influence. The aura of the Palace was enhanced by being directly on the Bosporus Straits on the European side overlooking Asia.

I loved the Bosporus Straits, the line between two continents. We took the family to Istanbul for a city break however, the kids soon got fed up with me as every opportunity we would take the ferry across the strait. I think we crossed over between the two continents at least five times but I loved the significance of it.

Sigiriya Rock – Sri Lanka

King Kashyapa (AD477 – 495) decided to build his new palace and fortress on top of a large rock. The King had made many enemies after killing his father and cheating his brother out of the Kingdom. So, he built a fortress where he would feel safe and secure.

The rock is enormous being 200 metres high and roughly 300 metres square. However, as soon I saw it – I knew there was a flaw. Where was your source of water?

As soon as his brother took revenge and killed the King the complex was abandoned due to the problems with water supply.

The climb up the rock was tough but the views over the surrounding countryside were excellent, including wild elephants in a nearby nature reserve. The layout of the palace was still intact because it had just been abandoned.

It was a stunning location for a palace/fort but totally impractical and, of course in those days if the King wanted to do something, it happened.

Mound of shells – Victoria Island

We took the family on a trip around Western Canada, in an RV, and whilst travelling through Victoria Island we went on a Whale watching trip. After the trip had finished the owner decided he need to refuel and took us through various inlets to a very small community (2 houses and a small pier) to buy fuel.

Whilst waiting we had a wander around and climbed a small grass hill next to the shore that was c40 metres high so we could overlook the sea and the surrounding flat land. This mound was the only raised piece of land for miles.

The boat owner informed us that this area was the traditional home of the indigenous people who live on fish and shellfish. The mound was built up of hundreds of thousands of discarded seashells which they had thrown away after processing them for food. Experts believe this occurred over thousands of years – which you could easily believe given the size of the mound. They also believe they either moved on or were wiped out c600 years ago, but no one really knows what happened.

It was quite humbling to think a community lived here – processing their food – for thousands of years in this beautiful but harsh landscape – and yet we know so little about them.

Milton Keynes UK
Ingram Content Group UK Ltd.
UKHW011038180224
438010UK00005B/78